From a Bonsai to a Pine Tree

How to love the unlovable in ourselves and others

Antonella Di Giulio

Dedication

This book is dedicated to Anthony Arthur Augustine, the master who inspired this transformative journey. Your unwavering support, guidance, and challenge pushed me to grow as a human being—from a wounded Bonsai into a tall and resilient Pine Tree. Your influence on my life and the lessons you imparted will forever be cherished and carried forward in my own journey of self-discovery and understanding. Thank you for being the catalyst for my growth and transformation.

Contents

Forward

In the last few years, my journey has taken a profound turn—a turn inspired by the teachings of Thich Nhat Hanh. This path transcends mere academia, my profession, and my role in society; it is a sacred internal pilgrimage, a mindful exploration of life's intricate patterns, and the gentle art of understanding and responding to them. As I stand before you today, I do so not as a scholar or as a musician, but as a devoted pilgrim, akin to a monastic disciple, embarked on a profound odyssey marked by the transformative power of personal growth and the deep healing of our innermost wounds.

Allow me to guide you through layers of words into a personal metamorphosis infused with the wisdom of Thich Nhat Hanh—a metaphorical narrative of my own personal experience that resonates with the essence of progress, resilience, and the extraordinary capacity to heal ourselves, irrespective of how relentless life's repetitive cycles and struggles may seem.

In the not-so-distant past, I, too, found myself ensnared in unyielding cycles—cycles that reminded me of the ceaseless rhythm of existence, where birth, suffering, and transformation are inextricably intertwined. Familiar patterns cast their shadow, and my responses remained unwaveringly steadfast and unsettling, yet not comprehensible. It was as though I were trapped in the unending cycle of sameness, which was hindering my own spiritual and emotional growth. Throughout this transformative odyssey, I encountered mentors in various forms, each bestowing invaluable lessons—lessons akin to the teachings of awakened masters.

In a lifetime, each one of us encounters a myriad of experiences and individuals who act as our teachers, though not always in the conventional sense. These teachers do not stand at a chalkboard or in a classroom; instead, they manifest as life's trials, problems, behaviors, and even as individuals who may cause us to experience struggles. It might be the guy who stole your car, the brother who insulted you, the person yelling at you. Or the kind person who is showing you the way, the one giving you hope, the one supporting you.

Sometimes we encounter them by chance. Sometimes we encounter them by choice and we might expose ourselves voluntarily to such Masters. Much like the Buddhist concept of the "Master," these life teachers guide us, some in an unexpected manner. They present us with challenges, adversity, and discomfort, pushing us out of our comfort zones and into the realm of self-discovery. These life teachers may challenge our patience, resilience, and adaptability. You learn to look at them with compassion, to breathe, be patient. It is through these trials that we acquire life skills that cannot be taught through conventional means.

We learn about perseverance, empathy, problem-solving, and the strength of the human spirit. They force us to look within, to examine our reactions, our fears, and our limitations. In doing so, they become mirrors reflecting our inner world, much like the introspection encouraged by meditation. I initially struggled to learn any of the lessons that were presented to me. I kept repeating mistakes over and over again, similar situations kept representing in my life. Until I realized that the key to spiritual progress did not consist in altering external circumstances or behaviors but in tending to the wounds that resided within my own consciousness, as those were the root of suffering.

Each of us carries our own unique wounds. These wounds inevitably shape our experiences, relationships, and self-perceptions. It is these very wounds that invite us to embark on the path of healing and spiritual growth by embracing our suffering with mindfulness, understanding, and compassion. Our journey is not one of striving for perfection but of nurturing our inner development, fostering self-compassion, and unearthing the unwavering strength that resides within our own self.

My gratitude extends profoundly to the several mentors and teachers who have graced my path, with a special acknowledgment to one of my Masters, Anthony, whose presence on my path clearly showed me the location of my inner wounds and forced me to embark on the sacred pilgrimage of healing—a pilgrimage guided by the mindful footsteps of awareness and compassion. It might be counterintuitive to most out there, especially to those who have never thought about their inner suffering. We tend to divide individuals into good and bad and yet that is unfair to most. Some of our traits might be healthy, some might be wounded (not "un-healthy": wounded, bleeding, in need of care and attention.

This journey, dear seekers, is an ongoing process, much like the gentle breaths of mindfulness that accompany us on our path to enlightenment. For some, the journey might be just an easy walk in a beautiful park; for others, it might be a race to get out of a dark forest. It is a journey that, once undertaken, leads to the ultimate liberation and transformation of suffering.

When the challenges of existence appear overwhelming, greet yourselves with gratitude, because they are opportunities to learn your lessons. Embrace obstacles with boundless mindfulness, compassion, and the same sense of interconnectedness that you would extend to all sentient beings. I say that to you, dear reader, and to myself.

May the wisdom of this path be a lantern that guides you through the darkest of forests, and may the healing and growth you experience become a source of light that illuminates not only your own journey but also the path of those around you.

With heartfelt blessings and gratitude for the transformative journey that lies ahead,

Dr. Antonella Di Giulio

Introduction

It was a beautiful morning in early fall, and I found myself on my way to a retreat at the Blue Cliff Monastery. I was excited about the opportunity to deepen my meditation and mindfulness practice and to spend time in the company of like-minded individuals. The retreat center was nestled in the hills of upstate New York, and the scenery was breathtaking. The warm colors of the fall season were making everything magical and welcoming. The air was crisp, and the sun was shining brightly, casting a warm glow over the landscape.

As soon as I arrived at the monastery, I began to feel a sense of calm and serenity enveloping me. The peace emanating from the monks and nuns, their smiles devoid of judgment, was priceless. I knew that it was just a temporary feeling, but it did not matter at that point. For quite a few years, I had been living on the edge, feeling like my breath was always too short for me to fully enjoy something as simple as breathing. A temporary break was truly pleasant for me.

The retreat was to last a weekend, and I was looking forward to immersing myself in the teachings of Thich Nhat Hanh, a Vietnamese Buddhist monk and peace activist I had recently discovered while searching for answers to my internal turmoil and struggled to deal with difficult situations. I had probably read about him before, but at that time, I wasn't ready to change my way of thinking, to challenge myself, and to embrace his life-changing principles. And so, I might have read some of his quotes and thought, "Ah, yes... the usual Zen philosophy." Yet now his teachings resonated differently within me.

During one of the sessions, the group was invited to share their thoughts and questions. A very common question among the participants had been: "How can I be peaceful and compassionate in a world that seems to be full of anger and resentment? How can I love the unlovable and still remain strong, compassionate, and emotionally solid?" One of the young nuns shared with us that, like Thich Nhat Hanh, she aimed to be like a pine tree on the top of a mountain, able to always be the most beautiful tree she can ever be, despite rain, sun, snowstorms, and anything else the world could throw at her.

She spoke with such grace and beauty that everyone in the room was transfixed. I remember her beautiful smile while she was talking to us and how she was shining in the darkness of a meditation hall.

Her words resonated with me deeply, and I was struck by the imagery of the pine tree as a symbol of resilience, strength, and beauty. In that moment, I realized that becoming like a pine tree was exactly what I needed in my own life. I saw myself as a big pine tree, green, tall, beautiful, standing on my own with sovereignty and dignity.

As the retreat went on, I started contemplating this metaphor more and more. I began to see how the pine tree could be a powerful symbol for our own lives. I started seeing myself as evergreen. The pine tree does not resist storms, the rain, or the snow. Instead, it stands tall and firm, rooted deeply in the earth. It is flexible, bending and swaying with the wind, but always returning to its original position. It is a survivor, able to thrive in even the harshest of environments.

The more I thought about it, the more I realized that becoming like a pine tree was exactly what I needed in my own life. I needed to learn to sit with and let go of negative emotions, the inner critic, the pain, and cultivate more a sense of inner peace and compassion for myself and others.

I needed to accept things as they are and learn to be present in the moment, rather than trying to control, ignore, or change these things. And I thought I needed to clear away the weeds and grapevines that I had accumulated over time and that stifled my growth and prevented me from becoming my true and authentic self. So I thought at that time.

When we think about a project, but we do not know exactly what we are doing, as human beings, we tend to think that things will be easy. "Just think that you are a pine tree and all your problems will be solved."

Right? Easier said than done.

The reality was that things were not as easy: it is not that you have "just" to do this and this and you will become as strong and magnificent as a pine tree. I realized much later - after I had already started thinking about my experience and about writing a book and after I was already working on myself and on healing my past wounds - that we are not little pine trees and we do not need to grow any taller. That only applies to young children. If we all were so fortunate to have big, tall, and healthy pine trees as parents

and we would grow in an environment that would
foster love, resilience, empathy, compassion, and
self-control, then we would only need to grow and
from time to time clean up our environment and make
small adjustments.

Adults who did not have that type of
environment have a different problem (and honestly, a
perfect environment does not even exist.) As adults,
we are rather bonsais: our roots have been cut,
mismanaged, traumatized, wounded, and mistreated.

Therefore, we grow partially well. Some of our parts are fully developed, some other parts keep bleeding and hurting. We might resemble an adult and mature pine tree from the outside. And partially we remain in a small, child-like type of behavior in our hurt roots on the inside. It has been a great realization for my own personal journey: This realization came to me suddenly during a short vacation in the Adirondack mountains.

I was walking among small, big, and medium pine trees. The tiny pine trees were growing just fine surrounded by their protective community of trees. And I realized then that we too could grow up just fine. Unless our roots are cut and manipulated by external events and circumstances. Mostly, by our primary caregivers, by our early environment, by extraordinary and unusually hurtful events. At that moment, I realized that I did not need to grow further, but to cure and heal the wounds of years of unhealthy encounters that had not been processed. I already was a pine tree. In a bonsai form.

In "From a Bonsai to a Pine Tree: how to Love the unlovable in yourself and others" I invite you to join me on a journey of self-discovery and transformation as we explore the metaphor of becoming like a mature and tall pine tree in our own lives. Through practical examples, reality inspired stories, exercises, and meditations, we will learn to let go of anger and resentment and cultivate love and compassion for ourselves and others.

In times of chaos and uncertainty, it's easy to feel overwhelmed and lost. We may feel like we are drowning in a sea of negativity and despair, struggling to find a way out. But just like the pine tree on the mountaintop, we can learn to stand strong and tall, even in the face of adversity.

Throughout the pages of this book, we will discover the power of mindfulness and how it can help us to stay grounded in the present moment. We will learn how to let go of negative emotions and beliefs, and cultivate a sense of inner peace and compassion through meditation practice and through our own breathing. We will explore practical techniques for dealing with difficult situations and relationships, and discover how to find beauty and joy in even the most challenging circumstances. All things I am learning and I will keep learning along you all.

Most importantly, we will learn how to embrace our own inner strength and beauty, shrink our inner critic, and enjoy our authentic self, just like the pine tree on the mountaintop. We too can weather any storm and stand tall and proud, no matter what life may bring. Out there, right next to you, maybe in your house, in your family, out in society, there is fighting and disruptions, and a lot of anger and suffering. How can you stay peaceful and be a strong and beautiful pine tree in a world which seems that is seemingly set up to create despair,

The Pine Tree on the Mountaintop

It was the height of summer, the air thick with humidity and the sun's rays casting long shadows across the landscape. As I stood at the precipice of a foreboding forest, a shiver ran down my spine, filling me with an unsettling sense of despair. The towering trees loomed before me, their gnarled branches reaching out like twisted fingers, an ominous invitation into the depths of the unknown.

Summoning my courage, I took a tentative step forward, my feet sinking into the cool, damp earth beneath me. In that moment, I believed that I possessed the bravery and intelligence to navigate my way through this enigmatic realm. I was very courageous, after all. But soon, the path I had chosen twisted and snaked, leading me deeper into a labyrinth of madness.

I felt like a sponge, absorbing not only the physical sensations of the forest but also the intangible darkness that pervaded the air. With each passing moment, my attempts to escape seemed to amplify the weight of the shadows that surrounded me. The more I tried to radiate light and joy, the more those efforts were stifled by the encroaching darkness. The grotesque trees closed in around me, their menacing presence snuffing out the light, leaving me in a desolate gloom.

Lost and disoriented, I yearned for solace and called out for help, but my pleas were met with silence. Undeterred, I continued to cry out, desperate for a sign of light in this forsaken place. My attempts to find help only echoed through the forest, accompanied by the rustling of leaves and the creaking of branches. It was as if the very essence of the forest mocked me, whispering assurances that contradicted the reality I faced.

"You are fine!"

"This is the light!"

Day by day, I found myself growing more intertwined with the pervasive darkness. It clung to me like a relentless specter, infiltrating my being. The forest's negativity seeped into every pore, saturating my soul with fear, anger, resentment, and envy. It was as though I had unwittingly opened a conduit within myself, allowing these malevolent emotions to flow in unhindered. I grappled with this inexplicable breach, unable to discern its origin or purpose. Giving in to despair, I confronted the notion that perhaps any form of release, even death, would be preferable to a life full of unloving contempt.

The forest, once a mere path to be traversed, transformed into an impenetrable maze of despair, its obsidian walls confining me to a fate I never anticipated. I became a creature lost within its depths, screaming for help.

"Help me out!" "Somebody, anybody… help me!"

 Yet, my pleas fell upon deaf ears, for the voices around me, those who claimed reassurance, were the same voices that propagated the darkness, rendering their words hollow and untrue.

As I journeyed through this twisted realm, an eerie sight unfolded before me. Shadows danced and writhed, taking on sinister forms within the gloom. Initially dismissing them as mere figments of my imagination, my heart sank as they drew nearer, revealing themselves as tangible entities. These strange creatures, with features unlike anything I had ever encountered, lurked in the murky depths of the forest, their presence unsettling and filled with malice. Their unblinking eyes bore into my very soul, while their razor-sharp teeth glinted in the dim light, betraying their sinister intentions. It was as though they reveled in my darkness and fear, relishing the prospect of my ultimate defeat and transformation into one of their own.

I desperately tried to flee, my legs propelling me forward, but the creatures were swift and agile, effortlessly surrounding me, following me, mocking me for my attempts to free myself. Their voices whispered in my ear, enticing me to surrender and join their ranks. Paralyzed with fear, I found myself unable to move or speak, a prisoner in my own terror.

In that moment of desperation and vulnerability, a realization dawned upon me like a bolt of lightning. I was not meant to be here, trapped within a realm that thrived on darkness. Summoning the last vestiges of my courage, I mustered a scream, directed not only at the creatures but at the very essence of the forest itself.

"I am not like YOU!" I bellowed, defiance ringing through the air.

Though fear still clung to me like a suffocating cloak, a newfound determination ignited within. I refused to succumb to the fate that awaited me: I did not want to become an insignificant, vile creature consumed by the insatiable hunger of those who reveled in darkness.

With every ounce of strength I possessed, I vowed to break free from the clutches of the forest, to transcend the suffocating shadows, and find my way back to the light. I felt like Dante, in his first chant of the Inferno, trapped in a dark forest, unable to find my way out. But unlike Dante, I had no Virgil to guide me through the darkness. I was alone, lost. I had to find a way out on my own.

Summoning every ounce of determination within me, I thrust myself forward, overpowering the creatures that sought to hinder my progress. I stumbled and fell countless times, my body aching from the bruises and scratches acquired along the way. But with each fall, I rose again, driven by an unwavering resolve to find my way out of this abyss. Through the tangle of branches and the labyrinthine twists of the forest, I pressed forward, guided by an invisible force that seemed to push me towards salvation. And then, like a divine gift, a glimmer of light pierced through the dense canopy, illuminating my path. It was a distant signal of hope, a symbol that whispered of a world beyond this oppressive darkness.

With renewed vigor, I pushed myself through the final cluster of trees, breaking free into a small clearing. The warmth of the sun bathed my face, caressing my skin with its tender embrace. It was as if the universe itself had conspired to offer me respite from the clutches of the forest. "This is where I belong," I declared, my voice filled with certainty and newfound conviction. The radiance that enveloped me was not just an escape from the creatures, but a testament to my inherent nature, a confirmation that I was not meant to dwell in the depths of despair.

As I cast a final glance back at the creatures, their grotesque forms melting into the shadows, a sense of triumph welled up within me. I had discovered my purpose, my mission in this newfound journey. It was not enough to simply evade the darkness; I had to actively seek out the light that had briefly embraced me. With this newfound purpose, I ventured forth, determined to explore the vast expanse of the world beyond the forest's suffocating grasp. I yearned to immerse myself in the purity of joy, to bask in the radiance of love and happiness that had eluded me for far too long.

The path ahead remained uncertain, fraught with challenges and obstacles, but armed with the memory of that warm light, I forged onward. I sought out kindred spirits, individuals whose presence could infuse my existence with the same warmth and luminosity. Together, we would navigate the labyrinthine maze of life, shedding light in the darkest corners and dispelling the shadows that threatened to envelop us.

No longer defined by the darkness that had sought to consume me, I embarked on a quest to reclaim my essence, to heal the breach that had allowed the forest's malevolence to seep into my being. Guided by the flickering beacon of light, I vowed to shine brightly, dispelling the shadows that haunted not only myself but all those who yearned for liberation.

The forest was but a chapter in my life, a crucible through which I had emerged stronger, wiser, and more resolute. And as I ventured forth, my footsteps resonated with purpose, echoing through the ages as a testament to the indomitable spirit that refused to be ensnared by the darkness. But let us pause the story for a moment, for reflections to indicate to you the path like a gentle breeze. As I invite you to explore the depths of your own experiences, I ask you to ponder upon the shadows that have cast their gloom upon your path.

Perhaps it takes the form of a broken relationship, where trust lies shattered like shards of glass. The gnarled branches symbolize the pain of betrayal, reaching out to ensnare your heart and soul, causing an ache that lingers long after the wounds were inflicted. Or maybe your forest is a labyrinth of self-doubt and fear, the trees mirroring the insecurities that have haunted your every step. They loom overhead, their twisted forms feeding on your confidence, their whispered voices echoing your deepest anxieties.

For some, the dark forest could be the suffocating grip of grief and loss, the branches extending like tendrils of sorrow, clawing at your spirit. The haunting figures that inhabit the shadows represent the memories of loved ones lost, their absence a constant reminder of the void that fills your heart. The dark forest, in its many guises, is a realm where despair threatens to swallow hope, where anguish resides and joy seems elusive. But just as the protagonist of our story found their way through the labyrinth, so too can you navigate your own trials and tribulations.

How does your own dark forest manifest?

....

....

....

....

....

....

....

....

....

....

....

....

I started searching…

It was a typical day in August when I found myself endlessly scrolling through the internet, searching for a way out of the darkness that had enveloped my life. I had been struggling with a loss of my own identity for quite some time through the exposure to quite a few challenging and very toxic and traumatic experiences, and I was desperate to find some respite from the constant turmoil within me. A reset for my emotions. A way to go as far as possible from the horrible creatures.

As I aimlessly clicked through various websites, I stumbled upon a retreat which was offered at the Blue Cliff Monastery. I had never heard of the Blue Cliff Monastery before. Something about that retreat caught my attention. It did not seem to me like one of those places where you just go with a lot of hope, spend a fortune, and then realize that you are just less wealthy after the retreat. The presentation on the website was simple, honestly humble, transpiring mindfulness. There were no promises of miraculous experiences.

I found myself reading through the description on the website with increasing interest. It felt as if a retreat in such a simple and yet insightful place could be a transformative experience, a chance to cultivate love, compassion, and understanding through mindfulness and meditation. Very simple things. And eventually, in the case it was just a fake place like many others, I could have enjoyed at least just a few days of vacation. Not too bad, after all.

As I read, I felt a glimmer of hope begin to spark within me. Maybe this was the change I needed, a chance to break free from the cycle of despair, self-doubt and struggles that had held me captive for most of my adult life. And so, I decided to take advantage of a short summer trip to visit the monastery for just one day at first. Without much thought, I began to prepare for my journey to the Blue Cliff Monastery.

I remember the drive vividly, the winding roads leading me further and further into the heart of the countryside. The air was crisp for the end of the summer, and I could feel more excited with each passing mile. As I pulled up to the monastery, I was suddenly struck by its serene calmness and natural and simple beauty. It felt like arriving in a place of peace right away and it was almost inexplicable.

I stepped out of the car, feeling a sense of peace settle over me. It was as though the worries and anxieties that had plagued me for so long had melted away in the face of the monastery's calm and tranquil energy. As I made my way toward the entrance, I was greeted by the smiling faces of monks and nuns, each radiating a sense of peace and welcome. They were all slowly and joyfully walking toward what I later discovered to be the main meditation hall. I immersed myself in the retreat's teachings, learning to embrace mindfulness and compassion in a way that I never thought possible. I sat in meditation, listened to inspiring talks, and participated in group discussions with other visitors.

As I was driving back home, I knew that something within me had shifted. I felt lighter, more at peace, and more connected to the world around me and to the entire Universe. The monastery had provided me with the initial tools and teachings I needed to begin my journey far away from the terrible creatures that had been haunting me for years.

A journey rooted in love, compassion, and understanding. And in my own breath. "Breath!" Our own breath is what connects the mind to the body. We breathe unconsciously, and yet when we focus our own attention on our own breath, we are able to stay grounded in the present moment.

Once home, I applied what I had learned during this short visit to my daily life:

1) Breathing: whenever my thoughts started shifting from the present moment, I would take a deep breath and reconnect the mind to the body.

2) Mindfulness bell: I downloaded a mindfulness bell on my phone that rings quietly every 15 minutes. It reminds me of stopping and being present.

As a starting point of your journey in becoming a strong and solid pine tree, how can you train yourself to stay in the present moment? Are there tools and strategies you can use to remind yourself to stay present? List at least two minor changes you can implement in your daily life that would help you in that direction.

1) ....

....

....

....

2) ....

....

....

....

I decided to deepen my practice and go back later that same month for a longer retreat. I wanted to stay strong and compassionate, no matter what life brings. During this second retreat, we learned about the practice of mindfulness and how it can help us cultivate inner peace and compassion. We also practiced walking meditation, sitting meditation, working meditation, and eating meditation. We were encouraged to observe our thoughts, emotions, and bodily sensations without judgment, and to develop a sense of curiosity and kindness toward ourselves and others.

I enjoyed being there, but I was struck by a powerful question that many participants asked: "How can I remain peaceful and compassionate in a world full of anger and resentment? How can I love those who seem unlovable while still staying strong and kind?" It was a question that resonated with me deeply, as I too had struggled with maintaining a sense of calm and empathy in any circumstances. As we sat together in the meditation hall, one young nun shared with us a beautiful metaphor that has stayed with me ever since. She spoke of wanting to be like a pine tree on the top of a mountain, standing tall and strong no matter what the world threw her way. Despite rain, sun, or snowstorms, the pine tree remains the most beautiful tree it can be. I remember her serene smile as she spoke, and how she seemed to glow in the darkness.

The image of the pine tree resonated with me deeply. It represented never changing strength, resilience, and beauty. I realized that this was precisely what I needed in my own life. Like so many others, I had felt overwhelmed by the challenges of daily living, whether it be personal struggles or global crises. But the idea of becoming like a pine tree gave me hope and inspiration to change.

As the retreat came to an end, I felt more grounded and centered than I had in a long time. Leaving the Blue Cliff Monastery, I felt a renewed sense of purpose and commitment to my mindfulness and meditation practice. I knew that there would be challenges and setbacks, but I felt confident that I had the inner resources to face them with strength and compassion. The image of the pine tree stayed with me as a reminder to stay rooted, resilient, and compassionate, no matter what life brings. That chance discovery on the internet led me to a place of transformation and renewal, a place where I could begin to heal and grow. And for that, I will be forever grateful.

Why a pine tree?

In the teachings of Thich Nhat Hanh, the pine tree holds a special place as a symbol of strength, resilience, and mindfulness and by reading several articles and listening to several of his talks, you might find out that the pine tree is used as a metaphor for how we can cultivate a deep sense of love and compassion towards those who we may consider unlovable while staying grounded in our own well-being. For some of you, this might be an easy task.

For some others, dealing with stressful situations might trigger old wounds to bleed.

Imagine wandering through the dark forest, feeling lost and alone. You stumble upon a majestic pine tree. It stands tall and strong, despite the harsh conditions of its surroundings. The pine tree's ability to survive, with its deep roots and flexible branches, is comparable to the importance of weathering life's storms with grace and adaptability. And yet, the question remains: how can we transform ourselves into a pine tree?

Now, I would like you to stop reading for a moment and to look deeper into your own personal story. What would it mean to you to become like a pine tree? What would be different? How would YOU be different?

....

....

....

....

....

Letting Go of Negative Emotions

Driving back home from a weekend-long meditation retreat, I basked in the tranquility that filled my mind. The retreat had been enlightening, deepening my understanding of compassion and the root causes of anger. The newfound knowledge filled me with a sense of purpose, love, and a desire to connect with others on a deeper level.

As I drove, my thoughts turned to a friend who was grappling with health issues, as well as our strained relationship. I longed to hear his voice, to offer comfort and support, to connect on a deeper level. I reached for my phone and dialed his number, my heart brimming with empathy.

"Hey, how are you doing?" I asked.

"I'm not going to answer calls or text messages while I'm working," he replied, his tone harsh and angry.

I was momentarily taken aback. I had expected his usual warmth and kindness, and his sharp words caught me off guard. Then, a smile crept across my face. This was a good decision for him, I thought to myself. My laughter triggered a sudden outburst of rage from the other end of the line. He hurled an offensive name my way ("Why are you laughing at me, you fucking cunt!"), his words stinging like a slap across the face. I felt the breath leave my body, my heart pounding in my chest. Fear gripped me.

I pulled over to the side of the road, my hands trembling on the steering wheel. Overwhelmed by emotion, I felt like I couldn't continue. It wasn't the first time he had treated me this way, but it was certainly not the first time his words had shaken me. I seem not able to get used to them and the more I forgave, the more he seemed to feel entitled to be angry at me without reason. He had developed a habit of mistreating me, and I had often tried to defend myself, but it often led me to a traumatic state of mind in which I felt like the victim once more. I felt as I only had two choices: fight or freeze. "Flight" did not seem like an option to me at that time.

I had always believed in the inherent goodness of people and in the power of empathy to heal even the deepest wounds. But as I sat there on the side of the road, frozen in thoughts of despair, the weight of the world bore down on me. No matter how much kindness and compassion I showed, it seemed that people would always seek to hurt me. I grew weary of being the target of anger and aggression.

For a while, I sat there, lost in my thoughts, grappling with my emotions. I was trying to find some fairness, explanation. I was ready to fight back, to defend myself against the world's injustices. I understood that violence was never the answer, but I felt trapped with no other recourse. I felt defenseless against the world.

Finally, I made a decision. I would confront him, demand an apology for the pain he had caused me. And he did apologize, but it was too late. At that point, I couldn't even hear or comprehend the apology; the pain was too overwhelming. The wound was already bleeding, and no words could ever make it right.

I attempted to focus on my breath, seeking the peace that had eluded me for so long. But the pain was too immense, the hurt too deep, the distress too huge. My mind was in turmoil, and I felt violated, stripped of my humanity, consumed by my worst fears. As I sat there, on the side of the road, alone and afraid, I realized that sometimes, the world could be cruel and unforgiving. But even in the darkest moments, I knew I had to cling to my compassion, my empathy, my humanity. It was all I had.

Desperate for validation of my feelings and perhaps some justification for his behavior, I reached out to my friend's sister via email, explaining the situation and my discomfort. I had always struggled to communicate with members of that family, and yet I had always been nice and kind to them, no matter what they were saying to me or about me. Her response hit me like a ton of bricks: "You are a fucking crazy bitch!"

Those words felt like a dagger to my heart, and in that moment, I contemplated giving up on life. I had expressed my distress to another human being, only to be met with more aggression.

It was too much to bear, atop all the pain I had endured in the past and amidst the suffering in the world. The more kind my answers to her, the more she seemed enraged. I questioned whether it was even worth living in a world where I had experienced nothing but aggression, pain, and suffering. How could I believe in peace and strive to be peaceful when I constantly found myself surrounded by anger and aggression? How could I defend myself by seeking peace without feeling foolish in the eyes of the world? I longed to walk in peace, but it often seemed that everyone around me sought war.

Taking a deep breath, I attempted to calm myself despite the ongoing distress. I was consciously redirecting myself on a path of compassion over anger, looking into this person's suffering. Just like my friend, his sister had also grown up in an abusive household, where anger was cultivated to feel powerful and in control. In that moment, I visualized the environment where anger, neglect and abuse were the only lessons to learn as a child. Acts of kindness were met with insults and threats. Compassion, emotions, and gratitude were perceived as signs of weakness.

Then I thought of a pine tree, resilient against harsh weather and strong winds due to its deep roots. Likewise, I realized that I could let go of my anger and resentment by nurturing deep roots of mindfulness and compassion, and by embracing the impermanence of life. Of course, it was easier said than done, especially when confronted with situations that triggered my deepest fears and wounds. I had been overwhelmed by a wave of anger and pain that threatened to engulf me. I felt attacked, misunderstood, and invalidated, and my initial instinct was to defend myself and seek revenge. But then, something shifted inside me.

I realized that the more I resisted the situation, the more I suffered. Clinging to anger and resentment only distanced me from my true self and my core values. I felt lost; I aspired to be like a pine tree, steadfast and resilient, yet I struggled to manage my own emotions. So, I embraced my pain. I sat with the pain. That was all I could do at that moment.

I could intellectually understand and even forgive the single behaviors towards me, yet I experienced profound emotional pain over time that transcended mere reactions to their angry behavior. I had gained a deeper understanding of compassion and its potential to transform the world around me. I was still uncertain about the path forward, about how to comprehend my own pain and suffering to become as unshakeable as a pine tree.

I recognized that this newfound purpose couldn't be easily applied to my life. I needed to nurture my inner being first, It was like a seed planted within me, and it became my responsibility to nurture it and help it grow. So, as I continued along the winding road, oscillating between the negativity that had surrounded me and the calmness of my new perspective, I whispered to myself: "Breathe." Then, when my thoughts returned to a negative stream of emotions, I paused once more and reminded myself to take a deep breath.

Can you think of a similar situation in which you had to face some unpleasant behavior that triggered your own emotional responses? How did you manage to regain control of yourself? And what could you have done differently?

....

....

....

....

....

....

....

....

. . . .

. . . .

. . . .

. . . .

. . . .

. . . .

. . . .

. . . .

. . . .

. . . .

As I pondered these thoughts about how to change my emotional responses to unpleasant situations, my mind wandered into the world of martial arts. It was a realm I had immersed myself in for several years, a domain that had bestowed upon me invaluable lessons in strength, discipline, and compassion. In martial arts, one doesn't merely learn to defend oneself or become a formidable fighter; it transcends physical strength. It's about nurturing inner fortitude and the ability to choose peace. It's akin to a dance, where every move is meticulously choreographed, and each step is taken with intention and purpose.

Much like in martial arts, when we train our minds to be robust and resilient, we can stand tall and self-assured in the face of adversity. It's like constructing a fortress, one that's impervious and unshakable, a sanctuary where we can seek refuge amid life's storms. The true beauty of martial arts lies in its philosophy. It's not about annihilating one's opponent but rather about neutralizing their aggression and averting harm. It's about empathy, understanding, and the pursuit of non-violent solutions that benefit all parties involved.

Similarly, when we look deeper into our own consciousness, we can unearth the root causes of our negative emotions. We can try to understand unmet expectations and the wounds that give rise to anger and resentment. We can learn to shed our fears and defenses, recognizing them as learned responses to past traumas, primed behaviors, experiences, and discover ways to forge deeper, more meaningful connections with others. It's like a pine tree, digging its roots deep into the earth, drawing sustenance and stability from the ground beneath. Day by day, those roots grow stronger until the tree stands tall and proud, unwavering in the face of life's storms.

As I drove, a sense of gratitude washed over me. I was thankful for the knowledge I had acquired and for the myriad lessons I had absorbed along the journey. Gazing at the world around me, I knew there was so much more to discover, so much more to learn. I acknowledged that it wouldn't always be easy. Anger and resentment can be formidable emotions to conquer, like the storms that threaten to uproot even the sturdiest of trees. We might feel justified in holding onto these feelings, particularly when we perceive ourselves as wronged or treated unfairly. I certainly feel that anger when wronged. Conversely, we may wrestle with guilt for our thoughts and actions. In either case, pain remains.

I started reorganizing my mind around the practice of becoming like a pine tree and embracing the unlovable. I started understanding that it didn't entail condoning bad behavior or ignoring the harm inflicted by others while remaining defenseless against their attacks. Rather, it did not even mean becoming "solid" and "unshakeable," but becoming resilient. It involved recognizing the humanity within both others and myself and acknowledging that we all partake in a shared pain that festers inside and spills outward because we erroneously believe that offloading our pain and causing pain to others will alleviate our suffering.

Sometimes, we think, "I have this pain, and I dislike it, so I want to give it to someone else." In doing so, we cause pain to everyone around us, yet we remain in pain, because, regrettably, the act of transferring pain only creates more pain, infecting us and the world in which we reside even more. Becoming like a pine tree and loving those who appear unlovable is a lifelong journey, fraught with challenges and opportunities. It demands courage, patience, and unwavering perseverance. It requires us to cultivate the garden of mindfulness within ourselves, to peer deeply into our inner wounds, to facilitate their healing, and to nurture compassion while learning how to shield ourselves from harm.

Even in the face of adversity, we can unearth beauty and strength, much like the pine tree that remains resolute amidst the storm. It serves as a reminder that we are not alone in our suffering and that we can always find support and inspiration from others treading the same path. It's a call to trust in our own capacity for healing and growth and to never relinquish our aspirations of peace and happiness.

As I pulled into my driveway, I was filled with gratitude. The journey may be long and arduous, but the rewards are immeasurable. By relinquishing anger and resentment and nurturing compassion and forgiveness, we can grow stronger and more resilient, much like the pine tree that stands firm in the face of a storm. We can recognize that love and compassion are the keys to genuine happiness and lasting peace.

TRIGGERS JOURNAL

Now, take a deep breath and commence journaling your triggers using a readily available tool such as your phone or computer. Reflect on the situations that trigger your emotional responses. Examine the memories tied to these triggers. Describe the emotions that surge when you are triggered. Consider the strategies that can anchor you in such moments. Focus not on the person or situation, but on your own feelings and on the types of situations or behaviors that activate your emotional responses.

The goal of this journaling exercise is to uncover the root cause of your personal pain, which may be unique to you, rather than to dissect the pain of another person or build a case against them. Remember that your aim is to become as strong as a pine tree on your individual journey of self-discovery and growth.

Lessons from the Pine Trees

It all began with a realization that struck me like a bolt of lightning, a realization that I needed to see, touch, and immerse myself in the very essence of nature to understand the profound lessons I had learned.

I decided to take a vacation to the breathtaking Adirondack Mountains with my children, a place where we could escape the chaos of daily life and find solace in the majesty of nature. As we climbed the rugged trails and inhaled the crisp mountain air, I was drawn to the towering pine trees that surrounded us. Their presence was both awe-inspiring and calming, and I couldn't help but feel a deep connection to these ancient giants.

As I walked among the tall pine trees, their branches swaying gracefully in the mountain breeze, I found myself observing not just their grandeur but also their relationship with the smaller trees that grew in their shadow. These smaller trees, often overshadowed by their towering companions, thrived in the shelter of the mature pines. They grew healthy and vibrant, protected from the harsh elements that could otherwise hinder their growth.

In that moment, some questions began to form in my mind, questions that would set the stage for my journey of self-discovery. I asked myself, "Am I already an adult, or like many adult humans, do I not feel fully grown? Could it be that, unlike these smaller trees protected by the mighty pines, I am already an adult tree, but have wounds and parts of myself that remain small and stunted, and this prevents my growth?"

As we continued our hike through the Adirondack wilderness, my mind became almost obsessed with thoughts of bonsai trees. I thought about how these miniature trees, although fully functioning in their almost-adult shapes, were intentionally kept small by the careful and deliberate process of root-cutting. The truth was that despite their outward appearance, their roots remained constantly cut, preventing them from reaching their full potential.

In my mind, I began to develop a profound analogy. Just as bonsai trees were fully formed yet perpetually small due to their ongoing root-cutting, I wondered if humans too were shaped by their experiences, with some parts fully functional and others remaining wounded and incapable of growing. It was a revelation that led me to ponder the complexities of human existence.

The realization struck me with a sense of urgency. I needed to explore this idea further, to understand how our past experiences, like the continuous pruning of bonsai roots, could affect our growth as individuals. It was a journey of self-discovery that would not only lead me to the lessons of the pine trees but also to the garden of bonsai within the recesses of my own mind.

As I continued my climb up the mountains, surrounded by the natural beauty of the Adirondacks, I couldn't shake the feeling that this journey would offer me profound insights into the complexities of human nature. I was determined to learn not only from the external world of towering pines but also from the inner world of the bonsai, where our deepest wounds and potential for growth coexisted.

With this newfound perspective, I embarked on the journey of discovery, seeking wisdom from the forest to guide me in both personal growth and building meaningful connections.

Lesson #1: Acceptance

The first lesson was acceptance. Just as the pine tree didn't resist the wind but accepted it as a natural part of its environment, I needed to acknowledge that not all relationships would be easy.

Some individuals carried their unresolved issues, and not everyone would be easy to deal with. Embracing this reality allowed me to approach difficult relationships with an open heart and mind, free from the compulsion to change or control others. Just as the wind blows regardless of our actions, we cannot control the actions of others. The wind simply is, and we must learn to adapt.

Lesson #2: Boundaries

The second lesson was all about boundaries. Like the pine tree's strong roots that anchored it firmly in the earth, I understood the importance of setting healthy boundaries in my relationships. It meant knowing when to say "no" when it was necessary to protect my emotional well-being and not allowing toxic people to drain my energy with their absurd and unjustified requests. Establishing boundaries, limits to others, became an act of self-preservation.

Lesson #3: Flexibility

Flexibility emerged as the third key lesson. Just as the pine tree's branches gracefully bent and swayed in response to the wind, I realized the importance of flexibility when dealing with difficult people. Being rigid and inflexible only led to more conflict and stress. Instead, I learned to be adaptable, open to different perspectives, and willing to compromise when needed. Like the branches that returned to their original position after bending, I found that flexibility allowed for harmony even in the face of adversity.

Lesson #4: Self-Care

The fourth lesson emphasized self-care. Like the pine tree that stood tall and healthy because it took care of itself, I recognized the critical importance of prioritizing my physical, mental, and emotional well-being in navigating difficult relationships and experiences. I committed to self-care activities that brought me joy and peace. Just as the pine tree shed its dead branches, I understood the necessity of letting go of what no longer served me.

Lesson #5: Perspective

The final lesson was one of perspective. As I gazed up at the towering pine trees, I gained a new outlook on my own life and relationships that had shaped my human experience. I realized that not all difficult relationships were worth my time and energy.

Just as the pine trees accepted the wind without trying to change it, I learned to evaluate my relationships and focus on those that were healthy and fulfilling. I embraced the notion that while change and healing were available to everyone, not everyone would embark on that path towards enlightenment or nirvana.

Sitting among the pine trees and with the bonsais in the back of my mind, I understood that, much like the forest, humanity was a set of growth, resilience, and beauty. We carried our wounds and scars, but we also possessed the capacity for transformation and healing. These lessons had become an invaluable part of my journey, infusing me with strength and clarity to confront the chaos in my life. I departed from the forest feeling grounded, renewed, and ready to face the world with a fresh perspective.

But my journey of understanding didn't end with the pine trees; it extended to the vast landscapes of the mind. In the mind's eye, the bonsai garden was a place of imagination and reflection. Here, the bonsai trees represented not physical entities but rather the symbolic aspects of our inner selves. Each bonsai within this mental garden symbolized the wounded parts of our self, those aspects of our being that had been affected by past experiences and traumas.

I recognized that acceptance, boundaries, flexibility, self-care, and perspective applied not only to external relationships but also to the relationship we have with ourselves. It was within the garden of our minds that we could tend to the bonsai of our own wounded aspects, nurturing them with mindfulness, compassion, understanding and patience.

Lesson #6: Tending to Inner Bonsai

Therefore, the sixth lesson was about tending to our inner bonsai. Just as in the physical world, our mental garden required deliberate care and attention. We needed to acknowledge the wounded aspects of our inner selves and work towards their healing and growth.

Lesson #7: Patience with Ourselves

The seventh lesson emphasized patience with ourselves. Healing and personal growth were processes that often unfolded slowly, gradually. We needed to offer ourselves the same patience we would extend to a bonsai tree, knowing that transformation took time.

Lesson #8: Finding Beauty in Our Imperfections

The eighth lesson celebrated finding beauty in our imperfections. Just as a bonsai tree's unique form held its own charm, our wounded aspects were part of our individuality. We could find beauty in embracing our vulnerabilities and acknowledging that they were an integral part of our journey.

In the garden of the mind, I understood that the lessons from the pine trees were not only about how we relate to the world around us but also about fostering a compassionate and nurturing relationship with ourselves. Just as the pine trees taught me to adapt and grow, I would continue to apply these lessons to both my interactions with others and the nurturing of my own inner bonsai.

Implementing the Lessons: A Plan of Action

With the inclusion of lessons from the inner bonsai garden, let's consider how to apply these insights in your life. Here are three small, actionable steps for each lesson:

Lesson #1: Acceptance

1. Practice self-acceptance by acknowledging your own wounds and scars without judgment.

2. Embrace the idea that your past experiences have shaped you, for better or worse, and that it's part of your unique journey.

3. Cultivate self-compassion by treating yourself with the same kindness you would offer to a wounded bonsai in your mental garden.

Lesson #2: Boundaries

1. Set boundaries with yourself, recognizing when it's necessary to say "no" to self-destructive habits or negative self-talk.

2. Seek support from therapy or self-help
    resources to help you establish healthy inner
    and outer boundaries.

3. Learn to protect your inner energy by guarding
    against self-criticism and self-sabotage.

Lesson #3: Flexibility

1. Practice flexibility in your self-perception,
    allowing room for growth and change.

2. When faced with inner conflicts or self-doubt,
    approach them with an open mind and a
    willingness to explore different perspectives.

3. Foster inner harmony by adapting to the
    changing landscape of your thoughts and
    emotions.

Lesson #4: Self-Care

1. Develop a self-care routine that includes
    activities aimed at nurturing your wounded
    inner aspects.

2. Prioritize self-compassion as a fundamental
    component of your self-care regimen.

3. Regularly check in with your emotional well-being and adjust your self-care activities to cater to your inner bonsai's needs.

Lesson #5: Perspective

1. Evaluate your self-perception and acknowledge the aspects of yourself that are healthy and fulfilling.

2. Practice self-reflection to identify areas of your inner self that require healing or growth.

3. Embrace the understanding that change and healing are available to all aspects of your inner bonsai, not just the external relationships.

Lesson #6: Tending to Inner Bonsai

1. Dedicate time for self-reflection and inner exploration to identify wounded aspects within your mental garden.

2. Develop a plan to nurture and heal these aspects, whether through therapy, self-help practices, or self-compassion exercises.

3. Remember that tending to your inner bonsai is an ongoing process, and it's okay to seek support and guidance along the way.

Lesson #7: Patience with Ourselves

1. Practice patience with your own healing journey, understanding that personal growth takes time.

2. Cultivate resilience by embracing setbacks as opportunities for growth and learning.

3. Celebrate your progress, no matter how small, and acknowledge the gradual transformation of your inner bonsai.

Lesson #8: Finding Beauty in Our Imperfections

1. Shift your perspective to appreciate the uniqueness and resilience of your inner bonsai.

2. Embrace your imperfections as part of your story and source of strength.

3. Recognize that your inner beauty shines through your vulnerabilities and scars, making you a more complex and beautiful human being.

With these lessons from both the external world of the forest and the inner world of the mind, you are equipped to navigate the complexities of life, whether they involve others or your own self. The wisdom of the pine trees and the beauty of the bonsai within your mind offer a holistic approach to personal growth and connection with the world around you.

The Ongoing Journey

As I descended from the Adirondack Mountains, I carried with me not only the breathtaking memories of the pine trees and the lessons they imparted but also the profound insights from the inner bonsai garden of my mind. The journey of self-discovery was far from over, but I felt equipped with the knowledge and wisdom to face the challenges and complexities of life with grace and resilience.

I knew that, like the pine trees and the bonsai, I was a part of the ever-changing embroidery of existence, with both wounded and thriving aspects. And in embracing this duality, I found a deeper connection not only to nature but also to myself and to the intricate web of relationships that defined my world.

With each step, I moved forward, ready to tend to my inner bonsai with care, to embrace the beauty of imperfection, and to navigate the winds of life with acceptance, boundaries, flexibility, and self-care. This journey was a lifelong one, an ongoing exploration of the self and the world, where every lesson from the forest and the mind was a steppingstone towards a more profound understanding of what it meant to be truly human.

And so, I invite you to embark on your own journey, to explore the lessons that surround you, both in the grandeur of nature and the depths of your own being. For it is in this exploration that you may discover the strength, resilience, and beauty that reside within you, waiting to be nurtured and celebrated.

Becoming like a pine tree wasn't about changing who I was, but it was about developing new skills and strategies in dealing with the world inside and outside of me. It was about learning to listen deeply with openness and to communicate effectively with myself and others, to put aside my own egoistic needs and desires, and truly hear the needs and desires of my own true self. Effective communication, I realized, required both clarity and compassion. And a lot of training. I needed to be clear in my communication, using language that was concise, compassionate, loving, and easy to understand.

As I drove away from the Adirondack Mountains, I looked back at the tall, majestic pines, grateful for the lessons they had taught me. The journey towards loving the unlovable in myself and others would be a long one, but I was ready to take it one step at a time, just like the pine tree's slow and steady growth towards greatness.

A Personal Journey of Understanding

In the heart of my journey of self-discovery amidst the wisdom of the forest and the lessons of the bonsai, I uncovered layers of understanding and self-acceptance that resonated profoundly with my own life experiences. The pine tree's transformation from an outcast to a symbol of love and understanding mirrored my quest to navigate the tumultuous waters of challenging relationships.

A Personal Journey of Understanding

Drawing inspiration from my own life experiences, I couldn't help but reflect on a particular chapter that had tested the limits of my patience and empathy. It was a challenging relationship with a colleague at work, a person who seemed like a relentless storm, their negativity and criticism resembling thunder and lightning. My initial approach was to steer clear, to guide my metaphorical ship away from the brewing tempest. However, much like an unyielding tempest, they pursued me with even greater intensity, making our professional interactions feel like navigating through treacherous waters.

Avoidance, I soon realized, was no solution. While I couldn't control the tempest itself, I could certainly control how I sailed through it. It was a lesson akin to learning to navigate through turbulent waters. As I consciously embarked on this journey of understanding, I embraced the role of a lighthouse, a symbol of light seeking to illuminate the hidden struggles within my colleague. Listening became my lifeline, like a sailor deciphering signals from a distant shore. I asked questions not to challenge but to genuinely understand, much like a cartographer charting uncharted territories.

The Transformation Within Difficult Relationships

Though the journey was initially challenging, I began to witness a transformation in our relationship. A ray of sunlight was piercing through thick clouds after a storm. My colleague, sensing my genuine effort to understand them, started to soften their tone and approach, like the gentle subsiding of winds after a tempest.

This experience reaffirmed a profound truth: navigating difficult relationships isn't just about survival; it's an opportunity for growth and self-discovery. It is not so much about how good or bad people are, but about how we personally relate to them and look for ways to make these interactions positively impact our own self-growth.

Much like a ship emerging from a tempest stronger and more resilient, I had learned that by striving to understand others and establishing clear boundaries, when necessary, we could weather even the most turbulent of relationships and emerge wiser and more robust on the other side.

Lessons from the Garden of the Mind

As I continued my introspective journey, the wisdom of the forest revealed to me that this understanding and openness wasn't confined to external relationships alone. It held true for the relationship we have with ourselves, within the inner garden of our minds.

In this inner garden, the bonsai trees symbolize the wounded aspects of our inner selves, influenced by past experiences and traumas. The wisdom of the forest and the symbolism of the bonsai trees extended beyond external relationships, applying to the relationship we have with ourselves within the inner garden of our minds.

Embracing Self-Compassion and the Unlovable Within

While the journey of understanding others was vital, I also recognized the need to extend the same understanding and compassion to ourselves. This process began with discovering the most unlovable part of myself, a wound buried deep within, much like the pine tree's initial prickliness. Having compassion for this unlovable part was the key to healing, much like applying soothing balm to inner wounds. It was a necessary step on the path to self-acceptance.

Discovering the Most Unlovable Part of Ourselves

I found that the most unlovable part of ourselves often remains hidden beneath layers of self-protection and avoidance, like the core of a pine tree shielded by its prickly exterior. These layers are crafted over years of coping with life's challenges without taking the time to proper heal our pain, creating a seemingly impenetrable shell.

It's not a simple task to peel back these protective layers and reveal the core of our inner wounds. It requires a willingness to confront our deepest fears and insecurities, much like a pine tree shedding its outer layers to reach the tender core.

To start this process, take a moment to reflect on the following questions:

- What emotions or thoughts do I consistently avoid or suppress?

- Are there recurring patterns in my life that seem to lead to pain or dissatisfaction?

- When do I feel most vulnerable or exposed, as if my protective layers are stripped away?

____

____

____

____

____

____

____

____

Having Compassion for Ourselves

Having compassion for ourselves, as imparted by the teachings of Thich Nhat Hanh, is not a luxury but an absolute necessity on the path to healing. This compassion is like offering a soothing balm to our inner wounds, much like a tree's sap can heal its own injuries.

In our journey towards healing and self-acceptance, we often encounter moments of self-judgment and criticism. These judgments can feel like salt on our wounds, exacerbating our pain. To counteract this, we must learn to treat ourselves with the same kindness and care that we extend to others.

Consider the following steps in practicing self-compassion:

1. **Mindful Self-Awareness:** Begin by simply observing your thoughts and emotions without judgment. Allow yourself to acknowledge your pain and suffering without trying to fix or change it.

2. **Self-Kindness:** Treat yourself with the same kindness and understanding that you would offer to a dear friend facing a similar challenge or to a child. Mostly, our wounds originated in childhood and it is our inner child who is suffering. Speak to yourself as you would to someone you care deeply about.

3. **Common Humanity:** Recognize that you are not alone in your struggles. Every fellow human being has internal sufferings, no matter

how beautiful and happy they might seem to you from the outside. Everyone experiences pain and suffering at some point in their lives. This shared human experience can help alleviate feelings of isolation.

4. **Self-Soothing:** Find ways to soothe yourself when you're feeling distressed. I have learned to breathe and walk. To go outside and feel every sensation. This can include engaging in calming activities, practicing deep breathing, or simply taking a moment to be still and present.

Healing the Most Unlovable Part of Ourselves

Embarking on the journey of healing requires nurturing and caring for the most unlovable part of ourselves, the part of ourselves we do not like and we would rather ignore, much like tending to a wounded plant. This journey can take various forms, and each individual's path is unique.

Seeking professional support through therapy or counseling is one avenue for healing, offering guidance and tools to navigate the complexities of your inner world. Journaling is another powerful tool, providing a safe space to explore your thoughts and emotions, like the fertile ground where a tree's roots find nourishment.

Engaging in self-help practices that promote healing and growth is equally vital. These can encompass mindfulness meditation, yoga, or even creative pursuits like art or music. The goal is to find the practices that resonate with you and create a space for inner transformation.

Take a moment to contemplate the following:

- What steps can I take to nurture and care for the wounded part of myself?

- Are there specific activities or practices that resonate with me for self-healing?

- Am I open to seeking professional support if needed, to gain additional guidance on my journey of healing?

____

____

____

____

____

____

____

____

____

Recognizing Interconnectedness and Acts of Compassion

As we embark on the healing journey, we're reminded of the interconnectedness of all beings, much like a forest where the roots of trees intermingle beneath the soil's surface. Our actions, even those directed towards self-healing, have a ripple effect on the world around us. Like the way a tree draws strength from the shared soil, our healing process can impact not only ourselves but also those around us. As we become more compassionate and understanding towards ourselves, we naturally extend this compassion to others, fostering a more compassionate world.

Consider the following questions:

- How can my journey of healing influence and benefit those around me?

- In what ways can I practice acts of
  compassion, both towards myself and others,
  as I navigate my healing journey?

- What small actions of kindness can I
  incorporate into my daily life to contribute to a
  more compassionate world?

____

____

____

____

____

____

____

A Deeper Understanding of Unlovable

While exploring more the concept of the unlovable within, I realized that it isn't solely about acknowledging our wounds and pain; it's also about understanding the origins of our self-perceived unlovability. Think for a moment about it: "self-perceived." It's like embarking on a journey to the roots of our suffering, much like a tree's roots seeking nourishment in the soil.

Exploring these origins is a delicate process, requiring patience and self-reflection. It involves revisiting past experiences, relationships, and even societal influences that may have contributed to our perception of being unlovable. It requires us to understand the reasons behind our "self-perception." Maybe it is not that we truly are unlovable, right? Maybe just because we actually feel that way and perceive ourselves as unlovable, we end up acting in the world outside of us in that same unlovable way.

To begin this exploration, take a moment to reflect on the following:

- Are there specific life events or experiences that have shaped my sense of being unlovable?

- How have societal expectations and cultural influences contributed to my self-perception?

- What insights can I gain by tracing the roots of my feelings of unlovability?

____

____

____

Compassion for the Origins of Unlovability

To truly heal the unlovable within, we must extend compassion not only to our present wounds but also to the experiences and circumstances that have shaped our perception of unlovability, to those individuals and situations who have influenced that initial perception. Maybe to your primary caregivers in your childhood, your teachers, your encounters in life. This process looks like the act of offering compassion to the soil from which a tree draws its strength and sustenance.

The journey of compassion involves revisiting past traumas and experiences seen through a compassionate lens. It means acknowledging the pain and suffering we endured and recognizing that, like a tree, we adapted and survived to the best of our abilities.

As you look into this aspect of your healing journey, consider the following:

- How can I practice self-compassion when revisiting past wounds and experiences?

- Are there specific memories or events that require special attention and self-compassion in my healing journey?

- In what ways can I offer understanding and forgiveness to myself for the strategies I employed to cope with past pain and challenges?

Healing and Transforming

The path of healing involves addressing the roots of our unlovability, seeking to transform the soil in which our wounds were sown. This transformation is a profound process of self-discovery and understanding, much like a tree's roots breaking through rocky ground to find fertile soil. As we grow, we might have taken the habit of modifying our memories and making them feel less scary.

It is very difficult to admit that, yes, our parents were not so great, that teachers might have been abusive, that siblings might have tortured us, that classmates were bullying us.

It is equally difficult to look honestly at our real memories and to cultivate compassion and understanding for those who might have hurt us. In this transformative process, we become like gardeners of our own inner landscape, nurturing the soil, planting new seeds of self-love and self-acceptance, and watching as they grow and flourish.

As you navigate this path of healing and transformation, consider the following:

- What steps can I take to transform the soil of my inner landscape, creating a more nurturing environment for my growth and healing?

- Are there specific practices or rituals that resonate with me in this process of inner transformation?

- How can I envision my journey of healing as a path towards greater self-acceptance and love?

____

____

____

____

____

____

____

A Journey to Self-Acceptance

Through this journey of compassion and healing, we can arrive at a place of self-acceptance, where the unlovable within no longer defines us. It's a journey that requires time, patience, and a commitment to self-discovery.

As you continue on this path, remember that you are not alone. Many have walked this journey before you, and many will follow. It is a life-long journey. Your healing has the potential to inspire others to embark on their own paths of self-discovery and self-compassion.

Now, take a moment to reflect on your personal journey:

- What insights or realizations have emerged for me as I've explored the concepts of the unlovable within and self-compassion?

- How do I envision my own path of healing and self-acceptance unfolding?

- What steps will I take to nurture and care for the most unlovable part of myself, and how will I extend compassion to both my present wounds and their origins?

- In what ways can my healing journey contribute to a more compassionate world, both for myself and those around me?

Feel free to use this space to jot down your thoughts, reflections, and intentions as you continue on your journey of self-discovery, understanding, and healing.

Discovering Beauty and Empathy

As I explored my inner self deeper and worked on my personal growth and on understanding my inner life, I started thinking about the world of music theory, about my teaching experiences, and about the myriad of interdisciplinary inquiries that fascinated me. I couldn't help but draw parallels between the concepts I had been exploring professionally and the stories of personal transformation I had witnessed.

One particular story stood out in my mind, a story of a student who had once found herself stuck in a swamp of self-criticism and a profound lack of self-compassion. Her journey of self-discovery and growth had been like witnessing from the outside the power of resilience and transformation.

Imagine, if you will, a young musician drowning in self-doubt, struggling to extend even the tiniest bit of grace or forgiveness to herself for the smallest of errors. It was as though she was trying to hold her breath underwater for an eternity, her struggle etched on her face, and the pain palpable.

I knew she needed a lifeboat, a lifeline to pull herself out of the murky waters of self-doubt and self-criticism. I introduced her to a new practice, one that required her to be more loving and compassionate toward herself and her own mistakes. "It is okay to make mistakes," I said to her, "we should actually welcome mistakes as tools we can use for our own development."

It was like handing her a rope to climb out of the abyss, offering her a fresh vantage point to breathe and find solace. At first, this practice was very difficult for her. It was like asking her to walk barefoot over hot coals - an arduous and uncomfortable journey. However, she persisted, taking small steps each day, gradually making her way across the metaphorical coals. And then, something magical happened.

The air on the other side was fresher, the sun warmer, and her heart lighter. She began to see herself through a lens of kindness and compassion, and it was as if a veil had been lifted, revealing her true beauty. Her transformation resembled a caterpillar emerging from its cocoon, evolving into a breathtaking butterfly. She had shed her old skin, like a snake, growing a new one, one that was more forgiving, more loving, and more accepting. And in doing so, she discovered the power of extending that love and compassion to others.

This transformation had a ripple effect, radiating outward and touching the lives of those around her. She became a ray of light, helping others find their way back to the surface. Being a part of her journey, watching her evolve from a struggling student into a strong and confident individual, was a source of immense pride. It became clear to me that loving the unlovable, including in it the parts of ourselves we struggle to accept, is a profound and transformative process. It's like taming a wild horse; it demands patience, understanding, and unwavering commitment, even when faced with difficulties.

As an educator and a musician, I've come to appreciate that some of the most challenging individuals can offer us the most profound lessons. They test our boundaries, our understanding of ourselves and of the world, they compel us to reevaluate our beliefs and biases, and ultimately, they help us evolve into more compassionate and empathetic human beings.

"Loving the unlovable" goes beyond a superficial perspective of focusing solely on a person's positive attributes while ignoring their flaws and wounds. It invites us to embark on a profound journey of understanding and compassion.

In the context of this concept, "unlovable" refers to the aspects of an individual that are often overshadowed by their wounds, insecurities, and difficult behaviors. These are the parts of them that may be challenging to love or accept, both for themselves and for those around them.

The heart of "loving the unlovable" lies in acknowledging and embracing these wounded aspects of a person, recognizing that they exist as part of their complex and multifaceted being. It means extending our empathy and compassion to these wounded parts, understanding that they are a result of past experiences, traumas, or circumstances.

By loving the unlovable, we choose to see beyond a person's external behaviors or defensive mechanisms. We peer beneath the surface to connect with their deeper essence—their vulnerabilities, fears, and insecurities. It is an act of looking past the prickly exterior, much like a tree's bark, to discover the tender inner core.

Loving the unlovable requires patience and a willingness to hold space for others as they navigate their own healing journey. It's about recognizing that everyone has a story, a history that has shaped them, and that their wounds do not define their entire being. It's an act of seeing the potential for growth, transformation, and healing within each individual.

Importantly, loving the unlovable doesn't mean condoning or ignoring harmful behaviors or enabling negative patterns. Instead, it encourages setting healthy boundaries while maintaining a compassionate stance. It is about saying, "I see your wounds, I understand your struggles, I see your unhealthy behavior, and I am still here to support your healing with compassion."

In essence, loving the unlovable is a profound act of human connection. It reminds us of our shared humanity and the universal experiences of pain, suffering, and growth. It invites us to be sources of light and healing in the lives of those who may have forgotten their own inner light. Through this concept, we learn that love is not reserved only for the easily lovable; it extends to the most challenging and wounded parts of ourselves and others. It is a testament to the depth of human compassion and the transformative power of love and understanding.

The Power of Empathy

Empathy, I've realized, is the key that unlocks the door to loving the seemingly unlovable. It's the bridge connecting us to others, allowing us to grasp their pain and suffering on a profound level. It's about putting ourselves in someone else's shoes, creating a space for healing and connection.

I vividly recall a moment when a close friend of mine was grappling with a painful breakup. She was heartbroken, unsure of where to turn. Instead of offering advice or trying to mend her situation, I chose to sit with her and listen. I became a sturdy tree, offering unwavering support, allowing her to express her anguish and sorrow. In that moment, I understood that sometimes the most powerful thing we can do is simply be present and bear witness to another person's suffering. To be a pine tree in a storm and to accept the storm.

Cultivating love. Empathy and compassion, I've discovered, is like nurturing a garden. It requires time, effort, and patience, but with the right conditions, it can flourish and bloom into something beautiful.

Whether as an educator, a mother, a partner, or a friend, I've learned that beauty can be found in the most unexpected places. It may be hidden in the gaps, waiting to be unearthed, just like love and compassion.

It might not always be readily apparent, but with mindfulness, empathy, and a willingness to show up for ourselves and others, we can learn to love the seemingly unlovable and craft a world infused with kindness and compassion. This is not always easy, but something we should adopt this as the basic strategy of living.

One of the most valuable lessons I've learned in this time is the ability to seek out the inherent beauty in everything, even when it's not immediately apparent. It's reminiscent of the tale of the ugly duckling, whose initial appearance was rejected by others, but as it transformed into a swan, its true beauty was revealed for all to see. We just need to give time and space to the ugly duckling to become a swan. And a chance to do so.

In some periods of my own life where I felt rejected and unlovable. Yet, I've come to understand that there is beauty in every individual and everything that exists. It necessitates a shift in perspective to see it. People, I've realized, are often like old, weathered buildings. They may seem rundown and dilapidated on the outside, but within, they hold a rich history and unique charm waiting to be unearthed. Just as the gruff and unapproachable person might be concealing a kind and warm heart, these old buildings may house hidden treasures within their walls.

To practice this mindset of loving the unlovable, I actively seek out beauty in all things, even in the most unexpected places. This practice is not about denying the existence of pain, suffering, or ugliness in the world; rather, it's a conscious choice to transcend these aspects by recognizing the beauty that often lies hidden within them. I take a moment to appreciate the intricate patterns on a spider's web, marveling at the delicate threads that glisten with morning dew. These simple moments of appreciation remind me that beauty can be found even in places where it may not initially seem to belong.

Of course, some things in the world are undeniably painful or tragic. Some experiences and situations may appear devoid of beauty: this practice is not about romanticizing or trivializing suffering; it's about fostering a mindset that allows us to hold space for both pain and beauty simultaneously. In the face of profound suffering, it can indeed sound 'insane' to others. Some may question how we can find beauty in the midst of hardship, and that's a valid concern. However, this practice doesn't suggest that we ignore or minimize suffering; instead, it encourages us to embrace a broader perspective.

When we actively seek beauty in all things, we are not denying the existence of pain but choosing to expand our awareness to include both aspects of the human experience. For example, when faced with a heart-wrenching tragedy, we can find beauty in the outpouring of support and solidarity from strangers around the world. In the depths of personal despair, we may discover the strength to rise, heal, and grow. This practice encourages us to see the multifaceted nature of life, where beauty and pain often coexist.

Ultimately, seeking beauty in all things is an invitation to approach life with a sense of wonder and curiosity. It's a reminder that even in the most challenging circumstances, there is an opportunity for growth, transformation, and the emergence of unexpected beauty. It is a testament to the resilience of the human spirit and the capacity for love and compassion, even in the face of adversity.

I've come to realize that beauty may not always be immediately obvious or easy to find, but it exists, awaiting discovery. It's like a treasure hunt, where the ultimate prize isn't the treasure itself but the journey of discovery and the new perspectives it offers along the way. Hence, I continue to seek out the inherent beauty in all things. With each new revelation, I am reminded that genuine beauty goes beyond surface appearances—it's a reflection of the soul.

And to truly see the beauty in othersone must cultivate empathy. Empathy is like trying on different shoes, walking in them to understand the pinch and the experience. It's a way to appreciate the uniqueness of each individual, to comprehend their struggles and celebrate their strengths. When I encounter a homeless person, I don't see mere adversity. I see someone who has endured hardships that I may never fully comprehend. I see someone who has weathered the storm and emerged on the other side, battered, broken, and yet alive..

It's easy to dismiss those who differ from us, to turn a blind eye to their struggles, and label them as nuisances, or worse. But that's not the path I would want to choose. I want to see the beauty in everyone, to fathom the struggles that have shaped them. It's like observing a mosaic, each piece unique and beautiful in its own right, coming together to form a masterpiece.

Empathy is the cornerstone of understanding and connecting with others. It's the bridge that spans the chasm of differences, allowing us to appreciate the mosaic of human experience in all its complexity. I've learned that through music, through life, and through our shared human experiences, we have the power to love and appreciate the seemingly unlovable. It requires a shift in perspective, a willingness to cultivate it, and a commitment to seek out the inherent beauty in everything and everyone. It is in these moments of transformation and connection that we find the true essence of our humanity.

Discovering Beauty and Empathy - Practical Steps

As we dive deep into the profound concepts of self-compassion, empathy, and finding beauty within ourselves and others, let's explore practical steps and suggestions that haven't been covered extensively in previous chapters:

1. Cultivate Gratitude:

- **Daily Gratitude Practice:** Start each day by listing three things you're grateful for. This simple exercise can shift your focus towards positivity and self-compassion.

- **Mentor or Coach:** Consider seeking guidance from a mentor or coach who specializes in self-compassion and personal growth. Their insights and feedback can be invaluable on your journey.

2. Deepening Empathy:

- **Read Widely:** Expand your empathy by reading literature that expose you to diverse cultures and perspectives. This can broaden your understanding of different life experiences.

- **Volunteer:** Get involved in volunteer work or community service. Engaging directly with people facing challenges can deepen your empathy and help you connect with their struggles on a personal level.

3. Seeking Beauty Mindfully:

- **Nature Walks:** Take regular walks in nature and practice mindful observation. Notice the intricate details of the natural world, from the patterns on leaves to the sounds of birdsong.

- **Art Appreciation:** Visit art galleries or museums and spend time admiring different forms of art and of human creations. Challenge yourself to interpret the emotions and stories behind the artwork.

- **Acts of Beauty:** Create moments of beauty in your surroundings. This can be as simple as arranging fresh flowers in your home or setting up a cozy reading nook.

4. Integration of Empathy and Self-Compassion:

- **Empathetic Self-Talk:** Monitor your self-talk and ensure it aligns with the empathy you extend to others. Replace self-criticism with compassionate and understanding language.

- **Empathetic Listening:** Practice empathetic listening in your personal relationships. Make a conscious effort to truly understand the emotions and perspectives of those you interact with.

- **Teaching Empathy:** If you have children or are in an educational role, teach empathy to the next generation. Encourage them to understand and care for the feelings of others.

5. Continuous Growth and Reflection:

- **Feedback Loop:** Establish a feedback loop for self-improvement. Seek feedback from trusted friends or mentors on how you express empathy and self-compassion.

- **Challenging Moments:** Embrace challenging moments as opportunities for growth. When faced with adversity or self-doubt, remind yourself of your journey towards greater empathy and self-compassion. Analyze those moments as lessons to be learned and look at them from a place of empathy and compassion towards yourself and others.

These unique practical steps and suggestions can help our transformative journey towards deeper self-compassion, empathy, and a heightened appreciation for the beauty within yourself and the world. Each of these steps brings a fresh perspective and a new layer of understanding to your path of personal growth.

Learning to Love Like a Pine Tree

In the heart of the forest, where the sun struggled to reach, a small seed lay nestled in the damp earth, yearning to sprout and flourish. It was a tiny thing, almost insignificant compared to the mighty trees that towered above it like majestic guardians of the woods. The seed felt small and insignificant, dwarfed by the grandeur of its surroundings. It longed to grow into something beautiful, to spread its branches and reach for the sky, but it felt inadequate. Day after day, it lay there, hidden and unnoticed by the world around it, its hopes and dreams buried deep within. But as time passed, the seed began to understand that its true potential lay within its unique characteristics.

It was not meant to be like the towering oak or the graceful birch, but rather, it was destined to become a majestic pine tree, with its own charm and beauty. The seed knew it must embrace its own destiny and fulfill its purpose. It gathered its strength and began to sprout, slowly but steadily. Its tiny shoots struggled to

break through the soil, but with determination and
perseverance, it succeeded.

    As it grew, the seed felt the warmth of the sun
on its surface and the gentle caress of the breeze on
its leaves. It revealed in the sound of the rustling
leaves and the sweet songs of the forest birds. With
each passing day, it grew taller and stronger, until it
was a proud and towering tree in its own right. Now,
the seed knew that it was not small and insignificant,

but rather, it was a beautiful and unique creation, meant to be exactly as it was. It stood tall and proud, inspiring hope and inspiration to all those around it, a symbol of the power of perseverance and the beauty of individuality.

In the midst of a dense forest, where the sunlight barely filtered through the thick canopy of leaves, stood a pine tree. It was not the tallest or the most graceful of trees, but it had a resilience that was unmatched. Its rough bark was scarred by the harsh winters and the strong winds that swept through the forest, yet it stood tall, unwavering. Its branches stretched out like arms, reaching for the sky with determination.

The pine tree's needles remained a vibrant shade of green throughout the year, even when the other trees shed their leaves and stood bare against the elements. Its evergreen foliage was a symbol of its resilience and unwavering spirit. It stood proudly, knowing its place in the forest, embracing its individuality. The pine tree had found its purpose in the forest. It was not envious of the towering oak trees that overshadowed it, nor was it jealous of the graceful willows that swayed in the breeze. It had come to accept itself for what it was, flaws and all, recognizing that its imperfections were what made it unique and beautiful. It had learned to love the unlovable, including its own imperfect self.

Just like the pine tree, the forest was filled with diverse trees of various shapes and sizes. Each tree had its own strengths and weaknesses, just like the people who walked the earth. Some trees were tall and mighty, while others were small and delicate. Some had leaves that changed colors with the seasons, while others remained evergreen. But it was the pine tree that stood out, with its resilience and unwavering spirit, a beacon of hope amidst the forest's challenges.

The pine tree had weathered many storms in its lifetime. It had stood strong against the howling winds that threatened to uproot it, and it had seen its fair share of winters, with their icy grip that tried to sap its strength. Its roots ran deep into the earth, anchoring it firmly in its place, and its branches flexed and swayed, adapting to the changing winds. It was a symbol of resilience, a testament to the power of embracing one's uniqueness.

In a world that valued conformity and perfection, it takes courage to be oneself, different, unique. It takes strength to stand tall and proud, embracing one's flaws and imperfections, and recognizing that they were what made each person unique. Just like the pine tree, people could find their place in the world and flourish in their own way. They could be proud of their resilience and beauty, embracing the qualities that set them apart from others.

And so, the pine tree continued to stand tall in the forest, its needles glistening in the sunlight that filtered through the leaves. It had learned to love itself, imperfections and all, and had found its purpose in the forest. It was a living metaphor for resilience and self-acceptance, a reminder to all who passed by to embrace their uniqueness and stand strong in the face of adversity. For just like the pine tree, they too could weather the storms of life and remain evergreen, their spirits alive and thriving.

As humans, we often find ourselves grappling with the challenge of loving those who appear unlovable at first glance. It's not always easy. It is surely easier to love them than to love our own imperfections. We may come across individuals who are prickly, distant, or hard to understand. They may hold beliefs or values that clash with our own, or simply exude an aura that rubs us the wrong way. But what if we could learn to love like a pine tree?

I have had my own personal experiences in learning to love the unlovable. One such instance involved a person I believed to be a friend but displayed sociopathic behavior. He compulsively lied, triangulated, and manipulated everyone into incredible stories. His own father and brother included. Unfortunately, he did the same to me. I am not sure how I was expecting this aspect to be any different towards me. I could understand where this person was coming from, why he would act that way, and even feel compassion and empathy. Still, I felt hurt that he could not change his behavior. I was a friend, after all.

I kept asking him, "Why? I was there and helped you avoid bankruptcy. Why are you stealing from me? Why are you inventing all these lies? Why are you causing me trouble?" I felt trapped in my quest for justice and fairness, expecting it from a person whose struggles were hindering his perception of the world. Back then, I had not realized that what was hurting me more were my unhealed wounds, my own perception of self, my own pain, and not so much the actions of another human being who could surely not behave differently or think any better in that moment. For him, I was no different from any other human being out there. Somebody he would exploit for his own interest and gain.

The more compassion I showed to him, the more upset he became. At one point, he even asked, "Why are you still being kind to me, after all I have done to you? You must be completely insane." What I did not understand back then was that while I was trying to change and better this person's life, I had neglected to look inward and investigate why I was feeling all that pain for his own actions. At that time, I could surely be kind towards him, much less towards myself. My only explanation was that I was probably perceiving all the pain this person must have inside. I did not realize that it was not his pain that was causing my suffering, but my own.

Because I did not understand the lesson the first time, life presented me with a second chance to finally learn a lesson, this time through the experience with a person I was deeply in love with and profoundly connected to. This person, who is still dear to me, was unable to see and accept love. Love meant for him being in danger. The more care and thoughtfulness I kept showing, the more the fear grew that I was trying to control him, to harm him, to make him sick. It was heartbreaking to me. It felt like being framed into a mold which only resembles you, but it is very far from who you truly are,

Instead of standing tall like a pine tree, firm in my own roots, all these accusations made me bend myself towards my wounds, made me feel unlovable to him and to the world, to the point that life had become meaningless. For months I kept having the impression that I was such a scary monster that I did not even deserve to live. I was being yelled, insulted, accused of the most horrible thoughts I never had. I felt defeated in my own being human.

These personal experiences taught me that sometimes the most unlovable actions of others are reflections of their inner struggles and that our own unhealed wounds can amplify the pain we feel. Learning to love like a pine tree means understanding that while others may display unlovable behavior, it often stems from their own inner turmoil. It also means looking inward and addressing our own wounds, so we can stand tall and strong like the pine tree, resilient and unwavering in our love and compassion.

So, if you're feeling lost or inadequate, remember the story of the pine tree. Embrace your individuality, stand tall and strong, and become like a pine tree, evergreen and resilient. Learn to love not only others but first and foremost yourself, flaws and all, for it is in that self-love that you will find the strength to weather life's storms and shine brightly in the forest of existence.

Practical Steps for Loving Like a Pine Tree

Self-Compassion:

Begin by showing yourself the same compassion and understanding that you aim to extend to others. Recognize that you, too, have imperfections and wounds, and it's essential to address and heal them. Practice self-compassion by speaking to yourself kindly, just as you would to a friend in need.

Deep Self-Reflection:

Take some time to look into your own experiences and emotions. Reflect on past situations where you found it challenging to love the unlovable, whether it's in your personal relationships or interactions with others. What triggered your reactions, and what can you learn from these experiences?

____

____

____

Unearth Your Wounds:

Identify any unhealed wounds or unresolved issues within yourself. These may be past traumas, insecurities, or fears that contribute to your emotional responses in challenging situations. Seek professional help or support from loved ones if necessary to address and heal these wounds.

Shift Perspective

Understand that people who display unlovable behavior often do so because of their own pain and struggles. Practice empathy by trying to see the world from their perspective. What might have led them to act this way? This perspective shift can foster compassion.

____

____

____

____

Set Boundaries

While practicing love and compassion, it's essential to establish healthy boundaries. Recognize that loving the unlovable does not mean tolerating abusive or harmful behavior. Define your boundaries and communicate them assertively but compassionately.

Seek Support

Reach out to friends, family, or a support group to share your experiences and feelings. Sometimes, discussing your challenges with others can provide fresh insights and emotional support.

Mindfulness Practice

Incorporate mindfulness techniques into your daily life. Mindfulness can help you stay present, manage your emotional reactions, and cultivate a deeper understanding of yourself and others.
How can you practice mindfulness in your daily life?

____

____

____

Self-Reflection

Take a moment for self-reflection. Find a quiet space where you can sit comfortably. Close your eyes, take a few deep breaths, and consider the following questions:

What unlovable behaviors or individuals have I encountered in my life that have challenged my capacity to love and show compassion?

What were my initial reactions to these situations, and how did I handle them?

Have I recognized any unhealed wounds or unresolved issues within myself that may have influenced my responses?

How can I practice self-compassion and address my own wounds to become more resilient in challenging situations?

What steps can I take to shift my perspective and cultivate empathy towards those who display unlovable behavior?

What healthy boundaries can I set to protect my well-being while still practicing love and compassion?

How can I incorporate mindfulness into my daily routine to enhance my ability to love like a pine tree, resilient and unwavering in my compassion?

____

____

____

____

____

____

____

____

____

____

____

____

Take your time to contemplate these questions and
jot down your thoughts and insights. Self-reflection is
a valuable tool for personal growth and
transformation. Remember that learning to love like a
pine tree is an ongoing journey, and each step you
take brings you closer to a more compassionate and
resilient self.

Starting with Self-Love and Extending Loving-Kindness

In my own life, I have come across a vast variety of individuals who are like sharp-edged rocks, jagged and challenging to hold close. I was always curious about my fellow human beings. But one person in particular stands out in my mind, as if etched into my memory with indelible ink. He was supposed to be my best friend. And he was a good friend for a while, until the mask of the nice and helpful guy started falling apart.

Our beliefs and values were like diverging paths, leading to distant destinations. Some of his values were utterly unethical, his ideas twisted and contorted, so far from what I considered right and just, or even just acceptable Our differences seemed insurmountable, like an impenetrable fortress, and I found myself constantly navigating through a minefield of frustration and anger whenever I interacted with them.

It was as if we were two opposing forces, repelling each other with a force stronger than gravity. Our conversations often turned into heated debates about why it is wrong to lie, our opinions clashing like cymbals in a symphony of chaos. I would try to make them see reason, to open their eyes to the truths I held dear, but it was like trying to light a match in a hurricane. The flames of my frustration would rise higher and higher, engulfing me in a blaze of fury, leaving me burnt and scarred.

As time passed, I began to realize that my anger was like a raging storm, blinding me. I was so focused on our differences that I failed to see the underlying humanity in them, the many wounds he carried, the struggles he had faced as a child being adopted by a family who cared very less about love. It was as if I was looking at a broken mirror, unable to see the reflection beyond the shattered shards.

Then one day, after many struggles, I realized that my need to be right was like a hunger that could never be satisfied, and my frustration was like a poison that seeped into every interaction, poisoning the possibility of understanding, but also my own life. I was like a captain steering a sinking ship, heading towards a disaster of my own making.

In that moment, I made a decision. I chose to let go this person and of my need to win, to prove my point. It was like lifting a veil that had clouded my vision for so long, and I saw them for who they were - a complex web of experiences, beliefs, and emotions, just like me. And in that newfound understanding, I found the capacity to forgive. It was not easy, and there were still moments when my frustration would rise like a tide, threatening to engulf me once again. Each time, I would remind myself of the journey I had taken, the lessons I had learned, and the person I had become.

As I look back at that chapter of my life, I realize that it was not just about learning to love the unlovable. It was also about learning to understand myself. Through my interactions with this person, I came to realize that my own need to be right and my rigid beliefs were limiting me, trapping me in a box of my own making. I had been so focused on external factors, on what others thought of me, that I had lost sight of my own inner truth.

I learned to embrace the unknown and the unpredictable. I began to discover a new sense of freedom. I found myself stepping outside of my comfort zone, taking risks, and exploring new perspectives with openness. It was like shedding an old skin and emerging as a new version of myself, one that was more open, more compassionate, and more alive.

My journey with this challenging person reminded me of the Japanese art of Kintsugi, the practice of repairing broken pottery with gold or silver, highlighting the cracks and imperfections rather than hiding them. It is a symbol of resilience, of finding beauty in imperfection, of turning brokenness into a work of art.

That is what this experience was for me - a chance to turn my brokenness into something beautiful. It was an opportunity to see beyond the surface, to explore the depths of my own humanity and the humanity of others. It was a reminder that love is not just about agreeing with someone or having the same beliefs, but about embracing the messy, complicated, imperfect nature of life.

In the end, I am grateful for the challenges this person brought into my life. Without him, I would not have grown in the ways that I have, and I would not have learned what it truly means to love and forgive. He was like a teacher, showing me the way to a deeper understanding of myself and the world around me.

As I move forward, I carry with me the lessons I have learned, the wisdom gained from navigating the rocky terrain of a challenging relationship. I am no longer afraid of the jagged edges or the sharp corners of life, for I know that beneath the surface lies a hidden treasure, waiting to be discovered.

The lessons I learned in the interaction with this difficult friend were like seeds that took root and grew into a towering pine tree, casting its protective shadow over my approach to other people. Just as the pine tree stands resilient, and adapting to changing seasons, I learned to stand firm and adapt my approach to different personalities.

Sometimes, difficult people might be like a tangled thicket of thorns, prickly and unapproachable. Their words and actions often let you feeling bruised and wounded, like thorns piercing my skin. But instead of focusing on the pain, when I find myself in these situations, I now decide to shift my perspective, like a skilled gardener trimming away the thorns to reveal the beauty underneath.

I try to look beyond our differences, like a bird soaring high above, seeing the bigger picture. I search for common ground, like a treasure hunter seeking a hidden gem. I practice empathy, putting myself in their shoes. I learned to listen with an open heart. There were times when I felt like giving up. But I drew on my inner resilience. People are not unlovable, but rather wounded and in need of understanding and acceptance, just like I was.

In the end, I realized that the lessons I learned from having compassion for my difficult friend were not limited to just that relationship. They had a ripple effect, shaping how I approached other people in my life. I now focus on what we had in common, rather than our differences. I learned to find common ground and build connections based on our shared humanity, like a skilled architect laying the foundation of a strong friendship.

I am grateful for the growth and transformation it brought into my life. It was not always easy, but it was worth it. Just like a diamond formed under pressure, my friendship with this person had turned into something precious for me and others. I emerged from this experience with a heart that was more compassionate, resilient, and open to embracing the unlovable. For in the end, I learned to love unconditionally and embrace the beauty of our shared humanity.

In your pursuit of loving unconditionally, consider the power of mindfulness and perspective shifts as invaluable tools. By incorporating mindfulness techniques into your daily life, you can anchor yourself in the present moment, gaining the ability to manage emotional reactions effectively. Mindfulness is like a gentle anchor, keeping you grounded amidst life's storms. It allows you to observe your thoughts and feelings without judgment, creating space for understanding and empathy to blossom. Practice mindfulness not as a fleeting exercise but as a lifelong commitment to staying present.

Make a deliberate effort to shift your perspective. Instead of dwelling on differences and disagreements, consciously seek out common ground and shared humanity. Imagine it as adjusting the lens through which you view others, focusing on the aspects that connect rather than divide.

Practice Active Listening

An essential component of loving unconditionally is the practice of active listening. To truly hear what others have to say is to embark on a journey of profound connection. Approach conversations with an open heart and a genuine willingness to understand. Active listening is a skill that requires patience and empathy. It involves not only hearing words but also deciphering the emotions and intentions behind them. When you actively listen, you create a space where people feel heard, valued, and respected. This act of deep listening lays the foundation for meaningful relationships built on trust and compassion.

Embracing Forgiveness

In your quest for unconditional love, embrace the transformative power of forgiveness. It is a force that can heal wounds, mend broken connections, and set you free from the heavy burden of resentment. Forgiveness is not a passive act of condoning harmful behavior; it's an active choice to release yourself from the chains of bitterness and anger. Understand that forgiving others is an act of self-compassion, allowing you to let go of the past and move forward with an open heart.

As you contemplate these principles, remember that they are not isolated steps but interconnected threads in the tapestry of loving unconditionally. They form the foundation upon which you can build deeper, more meaningful relationships, not just with others but with yourself as well.

Loving Unconditionally

Take a moment for self-reflection, as it is the compass guiding your journey toward loving unconditionally. Find a quiet space where you can sit comfortably. Close your eyes, take a few deep breaths, and consider the following questions:

1. How can I nurture and expand my capacity for self-love and self-compassion in my life?

2. What past wounds or life experiences have shaped my reactions to challenging individuals?

3. In what ways can I liberate myself from the need to always be right in difficult interactions?

4. How can I further develop empathy and understanding for those who challenge me?

5. What boundaries do I need to establish to protect my well-being in complex relationships?

6. How can I seamlessly integrate mindfulness and a shift in perspective into my daily routines, enhancing my ability to love unconditionally?

7. What concrete steps can I take to consistently practice active listening and open-hearted communication with others?

8. How can I actively embrace forgiveness, both for others and, critically, for myself?

Your self-reflection is a vital tool for self-discovery and personal growth. Through this introspection, you will find the wisdom and strength to embark on the profound journey of loving unconditionally. Remember that this journey starts with self-love and extends outward to embrace the shared beauty of humanity.

Navigating the Path of Self-Transformation and the Resilience of the Pine Tree

The journey of self-transformation is not a straightforward path. It's a winding road filled with unexpected obstacles and profound challenges. Along this journey, there are moments that put our capacity for understanding, compassion, and resilience to the test. One such moment in my life serves as a powerful reminder of the importance of tending to our own wounds and seeking peace and compassion, even in the face of the urge to react in dysfunctional ways.

Navigating the Path of Self-Transformation and the Resilience of the Pine Tree

Embarking on the journey of self-transformation means to set foot into a dense forest, filled with both the beauty of the unknown and the uncertainty of what lies ahead. It's a path of growth and discovery, but it's not without its challenges and obstacles. Just as the pine tree stands tall amidst the changing seasons and unpredictable weather, so too must we learn to navigate the ever-shifting landscape of our own personal growth.

The Courage to Begin

Embarking on the path of self-transformation demands a remarkable and unyielding courage. It's the sort of courage that beckons you to confront your own limitations, peer unflinchingly into the recesses of your being that may have long lingered in obscurity and set out on a voyage of profound self-discovery. This journey is a relentless quest of a pine tree's roots for sustenance deep within the earth and commences with a fearless exploration of your innermost self—a journey into the very core of your most hidden thoughts, emotions, and experiences.

In my personal odyssey, this courage was rigorously handed out to me during a deeply challenging relationship with someone who occupied and still occupies a significant place in my heart. Little did I anticipate that this individual would evolve into one of the primary catalysts for my personal transformation. I keenly recognized their struggles and their need for healing, and I tirelessly championed their quest for therapy and the introspective work requisite for growth. Yet, it became increasingly evident that they harbored a profound fear—a fear of confronting their own inner demons.

Rather than embracing the transformative process, they persistently sought refuge in a reality constructed upon the fragile scaffold of unresolved wounds—wounds concealed beneath superficial bandages. Their family's neglect and abuses were dressed by "love and light." Their actions and behaviors often left me entangled in a maelstrom of emotions, oscillating between hurt and bewildered confusion. It was within the crucible of this profoundly challenging relationship that I confronted a pivotal choice—to either shy away from discomfort or to summon the unwavering courage to confront my own wounds head-on.

Summoning the courage to face the immense pain that this relationship had ushered into my life demanded an extraordinary wellspring of strength and self-awareness. And of compassion and understanding. I had to summon the fortitude to confront not only the external dynamics but, perhaps more crucially, my own reactions, fears, and expectations. This marked my initiation into the profound journey of self-transformation—a moment of humble beginning, when the first fragile roots of a pine tree tenaciously penetrate the soil—a seemingly unassuming yet momentous step signifying the inception of an extraordinary path.

Retrospectively, I am profoundly thankful for the trials and tribulations that this relationship introduced into my life. It served as a crucible in which I was tested and forged—a crucible that ultimately served as the catalyst for my own growth and self-discovery. The courage to confront both external challenges and the complexities within ourselves is an indispensable companion on the path of transformation. It is the courage to confront not only our own shadows but also the shadows of others, recognizing that within these shadows lies the potential for profound healing and growth.

The Obstacles We Face

As we journey further down the path, we will encounter obstacles that may try to divert us from our course. These obstacles can take the form of self-doubt, fear, or resistance to change. They are like the storms that the pine tree weathers, testing its resilience. In our own lives, these storms can manifest as moments of self-doubt, where we question whether we have the strength to continue.

In my experience, one of the most significant obstacles I faced was the tendency to avoid discomfort and to try to give it away. When confronted with difficult emotions or challenging situations, it was easier to turn away and seek distractions, or to divert the attention to somebody else. I realized that I was spreading the metaphorical mud of suffering, trying to clean myself by avoiding the pain. It was like the pine tree trying to resist the winter cold by shedding all its leaves prematurely.

Learning to Sit with Your Pain

The wisdom of Thich Nhat Hanh offers guidance in such moments. He teaches that suffering is like mud we carry inside and inadvertently try to spread around to clean ourselves. Much like the pine tree enduring the harsh winter cold and biting winds, we too must learn to sit with our pain, tending to it until it heals.

In my own journey, this meant learning to sit with my own mud and the discomfort I felt in my challenging experiences. Instead of avoiding the pain, I began to acknowledge it, like the pine tree shedding its leaves in the fall. I recognized that the pain was a natural part of my growth process, much like the pine tree enduring the winter as part of its life cycle. By learning to sit with my pain and allowing it to settle, I uncovered hidden insights and resilience within myself, just as the pine tree thrives amidst the challenges of its environment. And if help was needed, I trained myself to reach out for help.

The Beauty of Resilience

Through the challenges and obstacles, we begin to understand the true beauty of resilience. The pine tree's ability to weather storms and adapt to changing seasons is a testament to its strength. Similarly, our ability to persevere through difficult moments and grow from them is a testament to our own inner strength. As we move forward on our path of self-transformation, we may stumble and fall, much like the pine tree facing strong winds. And it is ok. You should expect to fall over and over again. It is part of the process. But with each fall, we learn to rise stronger, our roots digging deeper into the soil of self-awareness and self-compassion. Our journey becomes a reflection of the pine tree's resilience, standing tall and unwavering amidst the uncertainties of life.

The Profound Rewards

Navigating the path of self-transformation is a courageous journey filled with obstacles and moments of discomfort. Yet, like the pine tree, we can learn to weather the storms, adapt to change, and embrace the beauty of resilience. By acknowledging our pain and learning to sit with it, we uncover the hidden gems of wisdom within ourselves, just as the pine tree thrives amidst the challenges of its environment.

The path may be challenging, but the rewards are profound, as we discover the strength and resilience that lie within us. As we persevere and grow, we become a living testament to the power of transformation and the beauty of embracing our true selves. The journey is not easy, but it is undoubtedly worth every step.

Embracing Change and Growth

One of the central themes of self-transformation is the inevitability of change, the impermanence of life. The pine tree, in all its resilience, teaches us that embracing change is a fundamental aspect of growth. Just as the tree sheds its leaves in the fall to prepare for winter, we too must be willing to let go of what no longer serves us in order to make space for new growth.

In my personal journey, I had to confront the fear of change and the discomfort of letting go. The relationship I mentioned earlier had become a comfort zone, despite its huge challenges. It was like the pine tree clinging to its old leaves because they were familiar, even though they no longer served any purpose. It was a reminder that growth often requires us to step out of our comfort zones and embrace the unknown.

Cultivating Patience

Patience is a virtue that the path of self-transformation demands. The pine tree's slow and steady growth teaches us the value of patience in our own journey. Change and growth do not happen overnight; they require time, nurturing, and resilience.

I often wished for quick solutions and instant clarity in my challenging life experiences. It was as if I expected the pain and discomfort to vanish with the snap of my fingers. I had to learn that transformation is a gradual process. It involves self-reflection, self-compassion, and a willingness to persevere, much like the pine tree enduring the seasons.

Celebrating Small Victories

Amidst the challenges and obstacles, it's essential to celebrate the small victories along the way. Just as the pine tree celebrates each new branch and each resilient stand against the elements, we too should acknowledge our progress, no matter how small it may seem. Celebrating small victories helped me stay motivated, grounded, and focused. Whether it was a moment of clarity, a breakthrough in understanding, or an act of self-compassion, each small victory was a step closer to transformation. It was like the pine tree's branches reaching for the sky, each one adding to its majestic stature.

The Power of Community

Finally, the journey of self-transformation is not one that we need to undertake alone. The pine tree is often part of a larger forest, where trees support each other through their interconnected roots. Similarly, seeking support and guidance from a community or mentor can be invaluable in our personal growth. I found solace and wisdom in connecting with others who had walked similar paths. Their insights and shared experiences were like the branches of the pine tree, providing shelter and guidance in moments of uncertainty. They reminded me that I was not alone in my journey, and that the collective strength of a community can be a powerful source of resilience.

The path of self-transformation is a courageous and rewarding journey filled with challenges, obstacles, and moments of profound growth. Much like the resilient pine tree, we learn to embrace change, cultivate patience, celebrate small victories, and seek the support of a community. The journey may not always be easy, but it is undoubtedly worth every step, as we learn to stand tall and resilient, just like the pine tree, in the forest of life.

A Journey of Self-Development and the Power of Peace, Compassion, and Loving Kindness

In the previous chapters, we embarked on a transformative journey of self-discovery and growth, drawing inspiration from the resilience of the pine tree and the wisdom of Thich Nhat Hanh. As we continue on this path, it is essential to analyze the practices and principles that can help us remain consistent and committed to our own self-development.

Walking in Peace

Thich Nhat Hanh, a revered Zen master and peace activist, offers invaluable guidance on how to walk the path of self-development in peace. His teachings emphasize the importance of mindfulness and presence in every moment. Just as the pine tree stands rooted in the present, we too must learn to be fully present in our journey.

Walking in peace means being aware of each step we take, each breath we inhale, and each thought that arises. It's about cultivating a deep sense of mindfulness in our daily lives. Thich Nhat Hanh encourages us to embrace the beauty of the present moment, for it is in the here and now that we can truly transform and grow, while accepting that we are not perfect infallible beings and therefore we will make mistakes. And it is ok. Nothing is permanent in this world: we change, we can do better.

In practical terms, mindfulness involves paying attention to our thoughts, emotions, and bodily sensations without judgment. It's about observing the flow of life within and around us. As we practice mindfulness, we become more attuned to our inner world and the world outside, enabling us to make conscious choices and respond skillfully to life's challenges.

The Power of Compassion: Extending It to Ourselves

Compassion is a guiding light on the path of self-development. Just as the pine tree provides shelter and sustenance to the creatures of the forest, we too can offer kindness and compassion to ourselves. Thich Nhat Hanh's teachings emphasize the practice of loving-kindness and compassion, known as "Metta" in Buddhism.

We often carry self-criticism and self-judgment, which can hinder our growth. Thich Nhat Hanh invites us to be gentle with ourselves, offering the same compassion we would to a dear friend. As we learn to love and accept ourselves as we are, we can then extend this compassion outward, embracing the humanity in others, even those we find challenging.

Self-compassion is not self-indulgence but a recognition of our shared humanity. It allows us to acknowledge our own suffering and respond to it with warmth and care. This self-nurturing attitude becomes the foundation upon which we can build our capacity for compassion towards others.

Loving Kindness Towards Others

Loving-kindness is a transformative practice that can profoundly impact our relationships with others. Thich Nhat Hanh's teachings encourage us to extend loving-kindness to all beings, including those we may consider difficult or unlovable. It's a practice of recognizing the interconnectedness of all life and acknowledging the suffering that others may carry.

In my own journey, I found that practicing loving-kindness towards difficult individuals was one of the most challenging yet rewarding aspects of self-development. It required me to let go of my judgments and preconceptions, much like the pine tree letting go of its old leaves. As I extended loving-kindness to these individuals, I began to see them through a new lens, one that revealed their shared humanity and the wounds they carried.

Metta meditation is a formal practice that involves repeating loving-kindness phrases to cultivate feelings of goodwill and compassion. These phrases typically start with oneself and then extend to loved ones, acquaintances, and even those with whom we have difficulties. The practice helps dissolve the barriers we've created in our hearts and fosters a sense of connection and empathy.

The Consistency of Practice: Integration into Daily Life

Consistency is the cornerstone of self-development. Just as the pine tree's growth relies on a steady and consistent process, so too does our own growth. Thich Nhat Hanh teaches that mindfulness, compassion, and loving-kindness are not occasional practices but a way of life.

To remain consistent on this path, it's important to integrate these practices into our daily routines. Mindfulness can be as simple as pausing to take a few conscious breaths during a busy day or being fully present during a meal. Compassion can be practiced by listening to a friend in need or extending a helping hand to someone in distress. Loving-kindness can be woven into our interactions with others, even in the face of challenging situations.

The Power of the Present Moment: Transformation Unfolds Here

Thich Nhat Hanh often speaks of the power of the present moment. In our journey of self-development, the present moment is where true transformation occurs. It's where we can observe our thoughts, emotions, and reactions with clarity and compassion. It's where we can choose to respond with kindness rather than react with judgment.

In my own life, I've learned to treasure the present moment as a space for growth and healing. When faced with challenging interactions or moments of discomfort, I remind myself to return to the present. I take a few mindful breaths, grounding myself in the here and now. This simple act of presence has the power to shift the course of an entire day and bring me back to the path of self-development.

Embodying Peace, Compassion, and Loving-Kindness

As we walk the path of self-development, we draw wisdom from Thich Nhat Hanh's teachings on peace, compassion, and loving-kindness. The journey requires us to be fully present in each moment, to cultivate compassion for ourselves and others, and to extend loving-kindness even to those we find challenging.

Consistency in practice is key, integrating mindfulness, compassion, and loving-kindness into our daily lives. The power of the present moment is where transformation unfolds, where we can choose to respond with kindness and understanding.

In the next and final chapter, we'll explore the culmination of our self-development journey and how it shapes not only our relationship with ourselves but also our connection to the world around us. Thich Nhat Hanh's wisdom will continue to guide us as we strive to embody the principles of peace, compassion, and loving-kindness in our lives.

A Testament to Who I Am Today - Embracing the Wisdom of the Pine Tree

As I stand at the threshold of this final chapter, it feels like a journey's end and a new beginning all at once. Today, I find myself reflecting on one of those days when the weight of the world felt like too much to bear. My mind had embarked on its well-trodden path, one that often led to self-doubt and uncertainty. It was on such a day that something truly magical happened.

In the midst of my internal turmoil, my daughter, with her innate wisdom, uttered a simple phrase, 'Mom, the pine tree!' Her words were like a ray of sunlight breaking through the darkest of clouds. They carried a power far greater than their simplicity might suggest. They were a reminder—a reminder of the journey, the growth, the resilience that had brought me to this point.

This chapter is a reflection, a celebration, and a glimpse into who I am today, a testament to the path I've walked, and the lessons I've gathered along the way. It's a moment to acknowledge the ever-evolving nature of life and self. Today, as I share this chapter with you, I'm not merely an author narrating a story; I am a fellow traveler on this path, one who has learned from the wisdom of pine trees, the resilience of the human spirit, and the unexpected sparks of insight that can come from the most unlikely sources.

My life has woven a narrative, a journey of self-discovery and transformation that mirrors the enduring wisdom of the pine tree. As I reflect upon this odyssey, it becomes clear that I am now a living testament to the profound lessons learned along this transformative path, a testament to the power of authenticity, resilience, change, and self-acceptance.

Embracing Authenticity

The journey toward embracing authenticity has been the cornerstone of my transformation. It is akin to the pine tree standing tall and unyielding, never seeking to mimic the other trees in the forest. Instead, it grows in its unique form, unaffected by the expectations and judgments of others. I too have embarked on a quest to shed the layers of societal conformity and expectations.

The path to authenticity has not been an effortless stroll through the woods. It has demanded patience, self-compassion, and unyielding resilience. Much like the pine tree's gradual growth, my journey towards authenticity has been marked by deliberate steps forward, interspersed with moments of doubt and introspection.

I've faced moments of uncertainty, questioning whether I was on the right path or whether I should succumb to the pressures of conformity. But I've always found a guide in the example set by the pine tree, standing unwavering amidst the changing seasons. It has been a reminder that, like the tree, I need not rush my growth. I've allowed myself to unfurl and evolve at my own pace.

Resilience and Self-Discovery

Resilience, a quality embodied by the pine tree, has been my faithful companion throughout this journey. Life's trials and tribulations have tested my resolve, yet I have emerged stronger with each challenge, much like the tree standing tall amidst the fiercest storms. Drawing inspiration from the wisdom of nature, I've recognized my place within the intricate web of life.

The trials and tribulations I've encountered have taught me the importance of resilience. I've stumbled and fallen, but I've risen with newfound strength, brushing off the dirt of self-doubt and continuing my ascent toward self-discovery. The enduring strength of the pine tree has shown me that, despite the setbacks and storms, I can stand firm and resolute.

Embracing Individuality

In a world that often encourages conformity and uniformity, my journey has celebrated individuality. Like the pine tree, I've grown resolutely, branching out in unique ways, and have discarded the pursuit of comparison. I've come to understand that each individual walks their distinct path, and mine is meant to be an extraordinary one.

Comparisons to others have been relegated to the past. I've realized that every individual treads a unique path, and mine is meant to be distinct. Just as the pine tree doesn't gauge its worth by the height it attains, I've learned that my true value lies in celebrating my individuality and thriving as my authentic self.

Resilience as a Guiding Light

Resilience, like that of the pine tree, has emerged as my guiding light. Life's trials have tested my determination, but like the steadfast tree, I have weathered the storms with more or less grace. Drawing strength from the wisdom of nature, I've realized my place within the intricate web of life, and

I've learned to navigate life's tempests with resilience and inspiration.

I stand today as a testament to the journey of self-development and self-love. I carry proudly the lessons I have gathered along this winding path, the resilience I have cultivated, and the enduring wisdom of the pine tree. I am a living embodiment of the transformative power of authenticity, self-acceptance, and the celebration of one's unique self.

A Universal Tale

My journey is not merely an isolated experience; it is a universal tale—a testament to the indomitable human spirit, the boundless beauty of individuality, and the timeless wisdom of nature. It is a testament to the extraordinary journey of embracing one's true self, a testament to the wisdom bestowed upon us by the enduring and magnificent pine tree.

In the universe of life, I am a testament to the enduring wisdom of nature and the beauty of individuality. I stand tall and proud, much like the towering pine tree, deeply rooted in my authenticity, and grounded in the profound understanding that I am unique and beautiful just as I am. My journey is not just my own; it is a universal tale—a testament to the indomitable human spirit, the boundless beauty of individuality, and the timeless wisdom of nature.

As I continue to evolve and grow, I stand as a living testament to the wisdom of the pine tree, a testament to the transformative power of authenticity, resilience, and self-acceptance. My journey is a testament to the enduring lessons of nature and the enduring strength of the human spirit.

Author Bio

Dr. Antonella Di Giulio (Ph.D.) is a visionary in the world of music theory, historical musicology, education, and interdisciplinary inquiry. With a PhD in Music Theory and Historical Musicology, she has spent her career exploring the intricate connections between music, semiotics, and linguistics.

Based in the United States, Dr. Di Giulio is the founder of Musica IQ, a groundbreaking semi-academic journal that provides a platform for music professionals to explore music related topics. Her journey in music extends beyond academia, as she holds a Master's degree in piano performance and is the proud owner of the Woom Talent Center, a renowned organization that provides training in music and in the arts.

Her journey is not confined to the world of music. Dr. Di Giulio has a unique perspective on life and relationships, which she has eloquently shared in her book, "From a Bonsai to a Pine Tree: How to Love the Unlovable in Yourself and Others." In this deeply reflective work, inspired by Thich Nhat Hanh's teachings, she draws profound insights from the natural world, merging them with her extensive knowledge to offer readers a path to personal growth and self-discovery.

Dr. Di Giulio's writing is marked by a unique blend of intellect and empathy, making her work not only enlightening but also deeply relatable. Her dedication to the arts and her commitment to understanding the intricacies of human existence make her a true luminary in her field.

As you journey through the pages of "From a Bonsai to a Pine Tree," you'll discover not only the depth of her knowledge but also the warmth of her soul, leaving you inspired to embrace your own path of growth and self-acceptance.

With her innovative insights, profound wisdom, and passion for the arts, Dr. Antonella Di Giulio continues to inspire individuals from all walks of life to explore the boundless dimensions of music, humanity, and the intricate interplay between the two.

From a Bonsai to a Pine Tree